D0787698

PERSONALITY PROJECTION

in the

DRAWING OF THE HUMAN FIGURE

Publication Number 25
AMERICAN LECTURE SERIES

A Monograph in
AMERICAN LECTURES IN PSYCHOLOGY

Edited by

MOLLY HARROWER, PH.D.

Research and Consulting Psychologist
New York City

Formerly Clinical Psychologist, Montreal Neurological
Institute, McGill University
Montreal, Canada

Eleventh Printing

PERSONALITY
PROJECTION

in the

DRAWING OF THE HUMAN FIGURE

(A Method of Personality Investigation)

By

KAREN MACHOVER

Assistant Professor, Emeritus
Department of Psychiatry
Downstate Medical School
New York, New York

CHARLES C THOMAS · PUBLISHER

Springfield · *Illinois* · *U.S.A.*

Published and Distributed Throughout the World by

CHARLES C THOMAS • PUBLISHER

Bannerstone House

301-327 East Lawrence Avenue, Springfield, Illinois, U.S.A.

This book is protected by copyright. No part of it
may be reproduced in any manner without
written permission from the publisher.

© *1949, by* CHARLES C THOMAS • PUBLISHER

ISBN 0-398-01184-2

Library of Congress Catalog Card Number: 49-7063

First Printing, 1949
Second Printing, 1950
Third Printing, 1953
Fourth Printing, 1957
Fifth Printing, 1961
Sixth Printing, 1965
Seventh Printing, 1968
Eighth Printing, 1971
Ninth Printing, 1974
Tenth Printing, 1978
Eleventh Printing, 1980

With THOMAS BOOKS *careful attention is given to all details of manufacturing and design. It is the Publisher's desire to present books that are satisfactory as to their physical qualities and artistic possibilities and appropriate for their particular use.* THOMAS BOOKS *will be true to those laws of quality that assure a good name and good will.*

Printed in the United States of America

R-1

ACKNOWLEDGMENTS

The author welcomes this opportunity to express her deep gratitude to her husband and colleague, Dr. Solomon Machover, whose stimulating discussions, encouragement, and guidance have been indispensable to the development of the method of drawing analysis that is here presented. The author is indebted to Dr. Sam Parker, Director of Psychiatry, Department of Hospitals, City of New York, for the unlimited use of hospital data in the preparation of this book. The author also wishes to thank Miss Raynor Ruth Tannenbaum for her devoted secretarial assistance.

CONTENTS

Part 1

PERSONALITY PROJECTION IN THE DRAWING OF THE HUMAN FIGURE
(A Method of Personality Investigation)

Part II

PRINCIPLES OF INTERPRETATION

Part III

ILLUSTRATIVE CASE STUDIES

PERSONALITY
PROJECTION
in the
DRAWING OF THE HUMAN FIGURE

PART I

PERSONALITY PROJECTION IN THE DRAWING OF THE HUMAN FIGURE

PROBLEM

In this book the writer will make an effort to outline a method of personality analysis based upon the interpretation of drawings of the human figure. That individuals reveal important aspects of their personality in drawing has long been recognized. What has been lacking, and I trust that the work that is now being done in drawing analysis will supply, is a degree of systematization of analysis of the graphic product which is at once comprehensive, communicable, and does justice to the intricacies of personality.

THEORETICAL CONSIDERATIONS
Phenomenon of Projection

Personality, we know, does not develop in a vacuum, but through the movement, feeling, and thinking of a specific body. Projective methods of exploring motivations have repeatedly uncovered deep and perhaps unconscious determinants of self-expression which could not be made manifest in direct communication. It is safe to assume that all creative activity bears the specific stamp of conflict and needs pressing upon the individual who is creating. The activity elicited in response to "draw a person" is indeed a creative experience, as will be testified by the individual who is drawing. Wide and concentrated experience with drawings of the human figure indicates an intimate tie-up between the figure drawn and the personality of the individual who is doing the drawing.

[4]

The Body as a Vehicle for Self-Expression

When an individual attempts to solve the problem of the directive to "draw a person," he is compelled to draw from some sources. External figures are too varied in their body attributes to lend themselves to a spontaneous, composite, objective representation of a person. Some process of selection involving identification through projection and introjection enters at some point. The individual must draw consciously, and no doubt unconsciously, upon his whole system of psychic values. The body, or the self, is the most intimate point of reference in any activity. We have, in the course of growth, come to associate various sensations, perceptions, and emotions with certain body organs. This investment in body organs, or the perception of the body image as it has developed out of personal experience, must somehow guide the individual who is drawing in the specific structure and content which constitutes his offering of a "person." Consequently, the drawing of a person, in involving a projection of the body image, provides a natural vehicle for the expression of one's body needs and conflicts. Successful drawing interpretation has proceeded on the hypothesis that the figure drawn is related to the individual who is drawing with the same intimacy characterizing that individual's gait, his handwriting, or any other of his expressive movements. The technique of personality analysis that is described in this book attempts to reconstruct the major features of this self-projection.

Constancy of Projection

How representative is a single drawing? What aspect of the drawing is distinctly and unalterably related to the basic personality structure of the individual, and what aspect is subject to conscious control and variability? In studying drawings (two or more) obtained over a period of time, it has been observed that structural and formal aspects of a drawing such as size, line, and placement, are less subject to variability than content, such as body details, clothing, and accessories. Whether an individual makes his figure large or small, where he places it on the page, whether he works with long continuous lines or short, jagged ones, whether the figure has an aggressive stance, whether it is rigid or fluid, what the essential proportions of the body are, whether symmetry compulsions are observed, whether there is a tendency to incompletions, to erasures, or to shading, are all features that refer stably to the personality structure. Occasionally, drawings of patients obtained over a period of years are so remarkably alike as to constitute personal signatures. Stability of projection is being further checked by experiments which are now in progress designed to validate the impressions gained from clinical use of the method. Sets of drawings are being obtained from the same subjects at stated intervals over a period of time.

Mood of Figure

In the act of translating the body image, or postural model in graphic terms, does the final product accord automatically with the postural and psychic tensions of the individual? Specifically, does the figure drawn appear happy, expansive, withdrawn, autistic, constricted, fearful, belligerent, affectionally starved? Does it appear vigorous or collapsed? Does it appear to be dominated by a specific organ complex? These are feeling tones or central trends and dispositions which, in the experience of the writer, reflect faithfully the tensions of the individual who is drawing. An experiment has been formulated in reference to this point. Subjects will be asked to draw a happy, sad, angry, or weak person. Subjects will further be asked to draw one figure which gives their impression of themselves and one indicating how they look to their friends.

Sources of Projection—Psychic Datum

The problem of how certain organs come to have certain meanings so that they could be communicated in the drawing of a human figure is a puzzling one. It suffices to say that, from the empirical standpoint, such graphic communications occur regardless of age, skill, or culture. One source to consider is the common social meanings that physical attributes tend to acquire in the course of social expression and intercourse. Thus certain body types tend to be associated with specific psychic attributes. The asthenic type is conventionally regarded as idealistic, physically weak, and refined, while the pyknic type is associated with earthiness and gregarious impulses. Expressions of anger, love, joy, and strength are common social images in terms of physical manifestations and motor tensions. Accepting the validity of these social images in no way commits one to accept the full theory of physique and temperament correlations. Our attitudes toward others and how we expect them to treat us are, however, in a sense, tied up with such physique-temperament correlations.

We tend to treat people of certain physical attributes in certain ways. A powerful physique will command submission. We ourselves are, in turn, encouraged to develop certain physical attributes if we wish to earn certain social treatment. The fact that we cannot escape the somatic entrenchment of our desires, conflicts, compensations, and social attitudes has considerable bearing upon the phenomenon of self-projection through drawing of the human figure. Studies to further validate the basic functional focus of interpretation in drawings are being made along the line of checking with individual subjects on the conventional stereotypes of meanings associated with body types. Subjects are being asked for their associations in regard to organs of the body, various clothing details and accessories. What does a large nose, a jutting chin, broad shoulders, thin lips or large hands denote?

In addition to the socially common language discussed above, psychosomatic correlation of body expression may rise out of the individual's own special experience, weighted with emotional valences that are specific to him. Special organs may acquire vulnerability to the extent, that they are the axes of the emotional life and adjustment of an individual. Examples of this may be seen in the oral receptive, concave type of mouth often drawn by the very dependent individual, in the stomach, which, in combination with the rectum, is an organ complex for the paranoid or homosexually conflicted individual, and in the attention often given to the neck by the individual who is severely disturbed about the interrelations of body impulses and mental control. In the sexually deviant, the specific organ concentration may assume erogenous emphasis in the drawings.

Another source of psychic datum consists in the symbol values that are projected in drawings. The objects most often treated with symbolic significance in drawings are the cigarette, the pipe, the gun, the cane, buttons, pockets, the hat, the hair, the nose and the feet. Efforts to trace successfully the meaning of the symbol to the individual drawing it, have been only fruitful with individuals whose unconscious is fairly accessible, like schizophrenics and persons in analysis. Interpretations of symbol values are in line with common psychoanalytic and folklore meanings.

These sources of the motivational, motor, and ideational patterns which contribute to the structure of the body image and thus render the human-figure drawing significantly expressive of personality are subtly fused in the graphic production. They have been isolated here for analysis and discussion.

In the production of a drawing, there emerges out of the individual's total experiential background a unique pattern of movement and idea. Its significance for personality stems from the fact that there are involved processes of selection out of the infinite pool of experience and imagery potentially available in combination with a dynamic organization of movement and percept.

The processes of selection and organization may take place with varying degrees of awareness and of directness. Most drawings contain elements of self-evaluation in both direct and compensated forms of projection and of both conscious and unconscious phases of self-revelation. Verification of the unconscious aspects may often be derived from a study of the clinical history of the subject, from the personality pattern reflected on other tests, and not infrequently from the subject's own associations to the drawings.

Illustrations of the Functional Basis of Motivation in Drawing

It is by no means assumed that when an individual sets out to make a drawing, he is at once overtaken by all the conscious and unconscious aspects of his body image. Some subliminal and determining process is involved, however, so that, for example, a sensitive, puny, undernourished subject finds himself impelled to draw a powerful ego-model with tremendous shoulders. In the same way, an obsessive-compulsive subject who expresses conscious wishes that he could ignore the control of his brain and be ruled by the raw impulses of the body and the brawn of his arms, does indeed draw a virile body with long ape-like arms, and a tiny head precariously balanced on this body. Another example of deep motivation is seen in the husky, alcoholic individual who gives a shrunken figure of a man with feet adrift in space, combined with graphic indicators of immaturity, guilt, and repressed aggression. Alcohol was indeed necessary to span the personality contradictions in this individual. We see then that drawings may contain an open confession of weakness and defect, a determined effort to compensate for defects, or a combination of both.

To illustrate further the predominantly psychological and functional focus of graphic projection—the basic rationale for drawing analysis—we may cite the case of the adolescent who, when asked why he drew pin-points for feet, promptly associated it with his own deep insecurity and inability to stand on his feet. We find another male subject omitting the arm from the mother-image figure, because, "she used to throw things," and the absence of the mouth being explained, "she used to curse."

In still another instance, the omission of the arm is explained, "because you might do harm with it," and a large head is drawn with the comment, "you can see what a brainy fellar he is." One subject complained that he is unable to draw the arms in any but a crooked manner, though he had good drawing skill. It is significant that this subject's main source of anxiety is the constant blocking of all contact and achievement by too much perfectionism and narcissism. The arm goes out to the environment with force and aspiration, but must indeed return to the body axis.

The projection of basic problems in striking graphic terms was further illustrated by the drawing of a male subject of nineteen who was undergoing the travails of a delayed adolescent crisis with conduct and emotional difficulties that added a schizophrenic flavoring. The patient was referred for hospital study because he had raped a ten-year-old girl. Examination found him a defeated, guilt-ridden and confused individual who attempted to cover up his immaturity, confusion, inner turmoil, and near-to-surface aggressions with a feverish effort to maintain active social communication. In his associations to the male figure, the patient indicated that the figure (and the subject himself) satisfies the needs of interpersonal relationships by a smile and a superficial social facade. The male figure is described as running to catch a bus (the direction of the running body is toward the "self" side of the page and is discrepant with the full-view treatment of the head.) The patient himself is confused, contradictory, and going in all directions at once. The most outstanding feature of the drawing is the castrated body which is represented by a single line and single dimension legs and arms, while the head is drawn large and facial features are articulated with the perfection, conviction, and over-detailing that suggest active fantasy. The patient does say that he wishes he were like Superman, and indeed the head does look like Superman. The importance of the head as a center of social communication and control is discussed later. For the present, it suffices to point out that the patient is expressing castration of the body with just a single line to represent it, while the head, which the patient regards as an indispensable and almost desperate front in his struggle against a sense of disintegration, is elaborated with fantasy detail. Fears of body disorganization may be referred to the patient's strong guilt regarding masturbation, his feelings of physical inferiority, religious prohibitions concerning the acceptance of body impulses, possible homosexual panic while in the army, and his present offense—rape of a minor.

The above instances can be multiplied a thousandfold, and represent only special aspects of drawings, but they will, I trust, in some measure, serve to communicate the functional orientation underlying the interpretation of drawing features.

Figures 1m and 1f — King and Queen — Man and Woman: The following drawings, done by a schizophrenic patient, are excellent demonstrations of the mechanism of projection and the levels upon which these projections occur. Although this detailed analysis of drawings is somewhat prematurely placed in the text, their richness of detail invites more than cursory consideration.*

---

* The reader is asked to bear with the brevity, specificity, and apparent abruptness with which some of the interpretation of drawing detail is offered. The author trusts that the rationale will be clarified to some extent with the reading of Part II.

Figure 1m (*top*) is the bust of a king, which the patient copied from playing cards while commenting, "Every man should be a king."

1m

The figure is imposing and space-filling. Not only is it a pompous bust, but it is put into a frame. The facial expression is one of harshness, austerity, authority, and penetration. The clothing, crown, and sword are drawn with

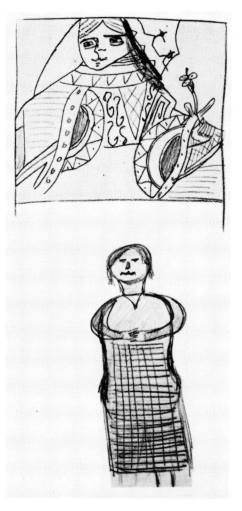

1f

heavy pressure and much detailing, representing material symbols of dominance and power. The hand is pointed toward the figure as if to call attention to the ego display.

A vast amount of emphasis is put upon the hair (*sexual*

virility) with almost dandyish development of the coiffure.

The chin cleft is indicated to suggest a determined chin.

If this drawing were done spontaneously, without copying, it would be regarded as essentially paranoid, grandiose, over-circumstantial, and obsessive in its characteristics.

The title, "King," was spontaneously written by the patient (*circumstantiality*), and indeed represents the wish.

In Figure 1m[1] (*bottom*) the male is represented as he really is—an homunculus who needs an armature to sustain him.

The figure is small, virtually "skin and bones" (*shrunken ego and sense of somatic disorganization*).

He is weak, is given effeminate curves for a body while wearing pants, and is given a poor excuse for a tie (*sexual inadequacy*).

The head is relatively large (*much ideational activity—seen in greater detail in the "King" drawing*). It serves to offset the depleted body.

Further, the separation between the control function of the head and the impulse life of the body is effected by an excessively long neck and a dark, double line cutting across the area of separation horizontally.

The arms which are short (*lack of ambition*), thin and weak (*lack of achievement*), are significantly placed above the body or "impulse" line, a point at which they can be better controlled.

The dark sticks for fingers suggest infantile aggression.

Clothing is indicated around the hips and trousers area in a manner suggesting homosexual panic. Further evidence of sexual agitation is suggested by a separate small line being inserted to close the open space at the crotch, and the light lines at the bottom of the trunk (*a sort of shading treatment marking furtive anxiety*).

The line, stance, and the middle placement of the drawing suggest overt aggression.

The facial expression is silly, shows forced amiability, and oral emphasis. The features of the face are treated in a simple manner common to childrens' drawings (*infantile social behavior*).

The hair (*sexual virility*) covers a large area of the head (*extent of virility strivings*) but is treated sparsely (*inadequate virility*).

The ears are disproportionately large and conspicuous (*ideas of reference, if not hallucinatory experiences*).

The midline (*preoccupation with somatic symptoms*) of the figure constitutes the main axis of the body. It is drawn with the emphasis and pressure to suggest aggressive conversions of body conflicts.

Buttons that adorn the midline (*mother dependence*) are in line with the patient's contrast between a weak, infantile man and a strong, authoritative woman figure.

In Figure 1f (*top*), we see the fantasy ideal of a woman—a "Queen." Figure 1f[1] (*bottom*), on the other hand, represents "Woman" as she really looms up in the patient's experience.

As with the "King," the idealized version is a pompous bust of a figure placed in a frame for display. It is overdetailed (*obsessive*), and overdressed (*conflict between body display and modesty?*).

We find a flower (*female symbol of reproduction*) indicated as contrasted with the sword (*penis symbol*) in the "King."

The "Queen" has excessive emphasis on the eyes

(*paranoid*) similar to the "King," but the expression in the eyes of the "Queen" is one of nun-like gentility in contrast with the sternness of the "King's" eyes (*a harsh father in the background?*).

Figure 1f[1] (*bottom*) features a powerful, hostile, castrating and rejecting female (*a mother-image that has probably saddled the patient with guilt and haunted him with disturbing infantile sex fantasies*). It is many times the size of the man and many times as powerful.

The hair (*sexual vitality*) covers a considerable portion of her face (*social front*). It is straggly and makes her appear drunk (*messed-up hair often associated with sexual immorality*).

The mouth is a compromise between a cupid-bow shape and a sneer (*lustful*), and it is drawn with much pressure (*aggression and sadism*).

The nose is shaded (*a castration symbol occurring in drawings of infantile males who project their defects upon the female*).

The body appears to have been drawn in the nude, and then shaded. Finally clothing was added in a compromise effort to conceal the transparency of the body (*voyeuristic trends, and anxiety shading*).

The outline of the pelvic region seen through the checks shows amplitude (*child-bearing fecundity*). The breasts, however, are barely indicated (*niggardliness in giving nourishment, ungenerous to children though she has the capacity to produce them*).

The arms (*contact features*) are short and folded (*rejecting*) but they are drawn with heavy lines (*powerful*) and shaded (*punishing*).

The outer contours of the body which extend over the

breast and pelvic areas are reinforced with heavy lines (*further evidence of conflict in mother-child relationship*).

The broad, thick neck of the woman contrasts significantly with the long thin neck of the man (*woman's better assimilation of impulses*).

The V neckline of the woman is drawn with a dark line (*sexual fixation on the breasts with voyeuristic trends?*) and accords with the transparency of the legs through the dress in interpretative significance.

The shading accorded the dress is dark and reflects a display of considerable psychomotor tension (*seen in drawings of sado-masochistic male patients who have been referred for sexual assault upon females*). Figure 1m[1] (*bottom*), the man, may be seen as the symbol of masochism while Figure 1f[1] (*bottom*), the woman, is the graphic expression of sadism in our patient's character.

The checked dress (*a form of rationalized shading*) covers all of the body area except the breast region (*less aggression focused upon that area than the lower parts?*). A dark, horizontal line at the waistline is given special emphasis in the crude criss-cross of the dress to mark the "above" and "below" (*additional evidence of strong sex consciousness*).

Transparencies (*break in judgment*) occur at such conflict centers as the position of the arms (*maternal rejection*) and areas of the body beneath the dark line marking the waistline (*voyeurism?*).

Coordination of the various features of all four drawings points toward the diagnosis of schizophrenia involving both hebephrenic and paranoid elements. The drawings do not represent a facetious presentation of an idea. They were done in all earnestness. It may be mentioned that in the writer's experience even artfully stylized and facetious drawings are incapable of escaping the projective implications relative to quite comprehensive aspects of the personality.

PREVIOUS INTEREST IN DRAWINGS

Clinical interest in drawings has in the past centered around theoretical problems regarding the relationship of genius to insanity and of the likeness of insane art to that of primitives and children. The literature records efforts to classify drawing characteristics in accordance with psychiatric groupings. These group descriptions were, however, so vague and overlapping that Anastasi and Foley (1), in their exhaustive survey of the literature, were forced to conclude that differentiations through drawings could only be made in the presence of extreme mental disorders and only with individuals who offer personalized, startling, or bizarre productions. Were drawings so limited in their ability to differentiate, they would offer no aid to diagnosis.

Enthusiasm for the revelations contained in drawings, revelations which could not be elicited by other methods of investigation, has been expressed repeatedly by many clinical workers. This enthusiasm did not, however, extend in the direction of codification or construction of principles of interpretation that would encompass the whole range of personality analysis. Interest in the possibilities that graphic expression offers for the understanding of the personality is now at its peak. Clinicians are collecting drawings everywhere, but the work done in drawing analysis seems to be limited to the clarification of particular problems relating to individual cases, to consideration of formal or structural features, and to the enumeration of isolated features common to special groups. Drawings as an instrument of comprehensive personality analysis must develop out of the study and understanding of the individual personality as well as analysis of group characteristics, and be referred to a basic and stable rationale. Drawings as a source for psychoanalytic associations have been described by Lewis (21), offering a context which should provide an excellent opportunity to validate some of the principles discussed here.

ORIGIN OF METHOD

The tentative principles of analysis presented in this discussion had empirical growth mainly in a wide variety of clinical material gathered in clinics and hospitals for mental observation over a period of fifteen years. Incentive for, and primary focus of, investigation centered around perfection of the drawing technique as a clinical tool for personality analysis, rather than around any theoretical hypotheses. In the course of administering Goodenough's Drawing-of-a-Man test for usual IQ purposes, it was discovered that careful study of the individual drawings often yielded rich clinical material not related to the intellectual level of the subject. Children securing the same mental age rating would frequently do strikingly different and individualized drawings. It was, furthermore, common experience to see socially inhibited, non-verbal children welcome the opportunity to unburden their private fantasies, their anxieties, and their guilt upon the objectified and impersonal figures which they drew and not be discomfited in the least by the thin transparency with which their self-portraiture was disguised. (See Figures 4m and 4f.)

The graphic communications of children proved to be of such clinical value, that drawings of the human figure were soon incorporated in routine clinical procedures and extended to adults of all ages. In the early stages, some timidity was encountered in eliciting associations to the figures from adults. Further experience with the technique indicated that the timidity was more a projection of the examiner's own awkwardness. The alacrity and fluency with which many sophisticated adults offer thematic elaborations contrast markedly with the poverty of their drawings and the strain with which they were produced. It is apparent that verbal patterns are symbolic, less direct, and more subject to conscious manipulation than graphic projection. Individual drawings were intensively studied in coordination with associations given by the subject and with relevant clinical data. On the basis of such study, formulations, and clarification of principles of interpretation of the graphic product have developed. Refinement, validation, and correction of these principles have been and are in constant progress. It is hoped that the exposition of the method here attempted will stimulate and in some measure serve as a guide for further research elsewhere.

EMPHASIS ON PATTERNS OF TRAITS

Except for the designation of isolated characteristics specific for the drawings of particular clinical groups, it is not intended, for the present, to construct a check-list of "signs" which can be used mechanically to establish differential diagnosis. Stress is laid primarily upon interrelated patterns of drawing traits as they may reflect the dynamics of symptom organization in a particular diagnostic category. Drawing traits tend to overlap in the same manner that symptoms in clinically differentiated groups overlap. As with the clinical use of all projective tools, grasp of mechanical details of drawing analysis cannot substitute for the knowledge of personality dynamics and clinical syndromes which is so indispensable to the proper use of the method.

Pathological and "Popular" Graphic Traits

The diagnostic import of a particular drawing feature depends upon its uniqueness or popularity. For example, if we consider the "conflict" treatment of hands and feet in a particular drawing (either in the nature of the preliminary remarks, omission, dimming out, erasures, shading, or reinforcement of those parts), we must be aware of the fact that it is a common drawing manifestation. The fact that it appears often in drawings does not deprive it of the interpretative significance generally attributed to that drawing feature. Disturbance in the hand treatment remains an indication of lack of confidence in achievement and in social contacts, while difficulties in handling the feet refer roughly to insecurity of footing. In our particular society, with its competitiveness and manifold contradictions, the uncertainties denoted by difficulties in dealing with the hands and feet of a figure are "popular." Thus, such drawing characteristics would not warrant the consideration of a neurosis in a particular case unless they are supported by other graphic indicators of maladjustment. On the other hand, when such drawing features as internal organs showing through a figure, or confusion of profile and full view of the head by any but a primitive subject are offered by an adult as a sober representation of a person, one has good reason to suspect the presence of psychosis. Bizarreness, excessive incongruity, over-symbolic treatment, and silliness are also specifically indicative of mental pathology.

Normality or Adjustment Indicators

Since the method developed in clinical context, it was natural that special emphasis should be placed upon indications of structural weaknesses and conflicts in motivation at the root of adjustment difficulties. The rich projection of the dynamics of personality that is found in drawings does lend the method to analysis of assets and constructive potentialities as well as to analysis of liabilities. At the present stage of the development of the method, evaluations in regard to adjustment capacities and degree of normality are made on the basis of interrelationship of personality traits contained in the drawing. The configuration of these traits is considered in terms of its clinical implications. No projective method can be expected to fully differentiate abnormality and normality without some reference to time, place and circumstances which might bear upon the value judgments that are derived from the test.

In a significant proportion of cases, drawings do permit accurate judgments covering the subject's emotional and psychosexual maturity, his anxiety, guilt, aggression, and a host of other traits. Whether particular manifestations of, let us say, sexual immaturity have led to, or will lead to particular difficulties in adjustment can be foretold with less certainty than the presence of that trait, because of the many modifying traits, and circumstances surrounding the personality. Normality depends upon the level of energy, the degree of control, capacity to integrate experiences, and most important, the readiness to face problems and defects. Drawing analysis of unselected so-called normals have revealed neurotic conflicts, anxieties, psychopathic trends, paranoid features, emotional, social and psychosexual immaturity, larval, and perhaps even full-blown schizophrenia. These judgments may even be well confirmed by competent observers who are acquainted with the specific subject. Some of these subjects may have kept out of clinics or hospitals because of factors extraneous to personality structure or dynamics. In short, the differentiation of normal from abnormal by means of drawing analysis is a less real problem than the effectiveness of the method in determining the personality and dynamics of the behavior of an individual—an effectiveness which could best be judged by verifying clinical analysis made by trained observers who employ similar concepts to those utilized by the drawing analyst.

In order to arrive finally at an estimate of adjustment, it is necessary to consider such factors as age, sex, mental level, cultural matrix, and the facilitation or stress of the environment. Adjustment ratings in reference to specific criteria have been found feasible with drawings, especially when "adjustment to what" is clearly defined. Although methods for weighing factors conducive to adjustment or normality are being studied continually, they require more specific research and elaboration if the drawing method be adapted more concretely for guidance and vocational selection.

PRESENT STATUS OF METHOD

The psychological orientation governing the analysis of drawings has already been indicated and will be discussed in greater detail presently. The principles of interpretation that will be outlined have received repeated justification and verification in clinical usage. Systematic analysis of the graphic characteristics common to specific clinical groupings is being undertaken in connection with the preparation of an extensive variety of clinical case studies. The writer has built up a fairly substantial file of drawings of all types with attached notes which give personal history, clinical data, and summary analysis of the drawings. These drawings are then classified in regard to many details of both the structure and content of the figures. In this way, particular drawing features can then be studied for specific meanings and for the groups in which they occur. Comprehensive personality analysis and diagnosis of unidentified individuals as well as of individuals whose clinical history is known have proved markedly successful. A number of these "blind" personality studies were in remarkable agreement with independent studies made on the same subject by Rorschach and handwriting experts. After years of experience with drawings, the writer is still enormously impressed with what people manage to communicate in drawings, regardless of skill or previous training. Prognostication of the course and treatment of a personality problem or mental disorder has frequently been accurately made solely on the drawings. Prognostic indicators may be more firmly established by systematically obtaining drawings at crucial points in the course of treatment.

An effort to match sets of anonymous drawings in groups of five with the appropriate case records was made in a brief experiment conducted by the writer and another competent judge. Neither the drawings nor records were previously seen by the judges. Although the clinical groups represented in each set of drawings were not too differentiated, a degree of accurate matching was achieved that was much better than chance. Research in the direction of validation and clarification of principles through study of individual drawings, clinical groups, and associations to drawings is in constant progress. Twenty orthopedic cases were studied for the possible projection of disturbances of the body image. The preliminary results were striking. Projection varied according to the basic personality of the individual afflicted, the degree of disability, and duration of disease, but important features of the subject's reaction to the disease were made graphically explicit in most of the cases.

To understand further the phenomenon of projection of special body problems which are realistically present, a study of the sensory handicapped is being planned to see if and how they regard the offending organs in graphic terms. It has been noted, in the course of clinical experience, that deaf people, or those who have had abnormal or disturbing auditory experiences, will most often give special attention to the ear. Narcissistic individuals who have never extended their libidinal energies beyond their own bodies will frequently give specific representation of the most minor body insult that may have occurred in their development. A barely perceptible and functionally insignificant polio residual was picked up in the drawing of one patient by a conspicuous reinforcement of the line around the right ankle. Most frequently the area of insult is indicated, but the type of injury cannot be determined without reference to personal history.

For a general study involving body image contrasts, it would be valuable to compare the drawings of dancers with, perhaps, those of architects or engineers, the body image of surgeons with that of psychiatrists. One would look for contrasts in postural models between primitive and ballet dancers, since the mode of dancing answers different needs.

Communicability of the Method

Clinical use of the method is best reserved for advanced workers. Seminars, lectures to professional groups, and considerable personal guidance in the method, given to a number of clinical workers, have spread familiarity with the technique widely, although there has been no previous publication. The method has earned a place of importance in the testing program of many progressive clinical units throughout the country. The dramatic nature of the method, ease of administration, and the direct method of interpreting from the figure, tend to encourage the novitiate to make dogmatic use of fragmentary knowledge. The writer has guarded carefully against popularization for this reason. With the proper training and experience, however, facility in the use of the method may be gained in a relatively brief time. It has been the experience of the writer that graduate psychology students have been able to acquire a grasp of basic principles involved in the method after some orientation lectures were given them.

Economy of the Method

The average time required for the drawing of the two figures falls between ten to twenty minutes. If associations to the figure are obtained, another ten to twenty minutes may be added. Equipment consists of only paper and pencil. The method may be adapted to groups, if the subjects do not work too closely together, offering a technique suitable to screening of problems in an educational, industrial, or therapeutic set-up. The approximate time that the writer requires to make a brief interpretation, sketching salient characteristics, is ten to fifteen minutes. This has not been checked with other workers. Comprehensive and organized personality descriptions take more time, but considerable saving of energy and time is effected by working directly from the product, rather than scoring or symbol values. It may, in the future, be necessary to develop some system of scoring for purposes of teaching, but for the present it has been found most fruitful to deal directly with the figure for interpretation.

ADMINISTRATION

The present technique of administration, after some revision, is simply to ask the subject to "draw a person." The subject is given a paper, preferably letter-size (8½" x 11"). and a pencil of medium-soft lead with an eraser. Observation of the drawing is made as inconspicuous as possible. Identifying data, preliminary questions of the subject, approximate time, sequence of the parts drawn, and spontaneous comments are noted on another sheet, and note is made as to which of the sexes was drawn first. When one drawing is completed, the subject is given the blank side of the page on which the examiner's notes on the first drawing were made, and is instructed to draw the other sex with, "now draw a man," or "now draw a woman," as the case may be. The directions to draw a "female" or a "male" have most often been used to prevent any specific definition of the figure that is asked for, since the subject may wish to draw a girl or a boy rather than an adult man or woman. In dealing with very young children it may be preferable to ask them to "draw somebody." The phrase that will permit the greatest freedom of projection has not yet been determined. If a head is offered as a completed figure, the subject is generally urged to complete the drawing. Whenever possible, both drawings should be obtained, but, if there is time for only one drawing, it is preferable that the subject draw the figure of his own sex. Resistance to drawing, which is encountered less as the examiner becomes more experienced and confident, can easily be overcome by assurance to the subject that the task is primarily of experimental interest, and has no relationship to skill in drawing. The subject is told, "This has nothing to do with your ability to draw. I am interested in how you *try* to make a person." If the subject omits an essential part of the body, he may be pressed into trying to draw that part after note of the omission has been made, to see if a clue can be obtained as to why he resisted drawing that part.

ASSOCIATIONS

Although of only supplementary significance to interpretation, associations are valuable for elucidation of individual meanings and specific problems involved in a drawing. The use of associations also furnishes an excellent

method of indirect interview. Most subjects pay little
attention to the graphic model while giving associations
to a drawn figure. They rapidly slip into their own defects, compensations, and wishful thinking. Personalization
is introduced often not too consciously and in thinly disguised forms. Actual use of the pronoun "I" may be
interspersed unconsciously. A fairly routine set of questions (see Table 1) designed to elicit the subject's attitude
toward himself and toward others is used. These questions
are printed on the side of the page which is used for the
examiner's notations. The subject is instructed, "Let's
make up a story about this person as if he were a character
in a novel or a play." If the subject resists, he may be
started off by the examiner with: "About how old does he
seem to be?" "Does he look like a married man?" In this
way he is being assisted by the interested participation of
the examiner, until he warms up to the figure. Some of
the questions are: "How old is the person drawn?" "What
is his occupation?" "Is he married?" "How much schooling has he had?" "Is he bright?" "Is he good looking?" "Is
he strong?" "What is the best part of his body, and why?"
"What is the worst part of his body, and why?" "Is he
nervous?" "What gets him angry?" "What are his worst
habits?" "What are his main wishes?" A brief series of
questions relating to the subject's social and sexual attitudes
are included. The subject is then asked if the figure reminds him of anyone in particular, and would he like to
be like the person drawn, or would he like to marry that
kind of a person. He is further asked to identify which of

NOTE: All questions to be adjusted for age and sex of subject. Positive answers
of clinical interest should be followed out in inquiry. Mark doubtful features of figure
or clothes on the drawing. Mark which drawing was done first by encircling the "M"
or the "F" with an appropriate "1" or "2" depending upon the order drawn; i.e.,
"Ⓜ – F; ① – 2" indicates the male was drawn first. Ask the subject whether any of
the traits described for either character may be similar to his (or hers).

ASSOCIATIONS

TABLE I

MACHOVER FIGURE DRAWING TEST — ASSOCIATIONS

Name.................................... Age........... Date...................... No................M-F:1-2

Problem.. Diagnosis...

(Make a Drawing of a Person) Remarks and Procedure......................................

....

....

....

Associations

(Doing).. (Age)............... (Married)..................

(Children)................................... (Live with)............... (More attached to)..............

(Brothers or sisters)... (Kind of work).........................

(Schooling).. (Ambition)...............................

(Smart)................................ (Strong)...................... (Healthy)..............................

(Good looking)........................ (Best part)...................... (Worst part).........................

(Nervous type).. (What's on his mind)...

(Fears).. (Sad or happy)....................................

(What gets him angry)....................................... (Wish for most)...............................

(Good points).. (Bad points)...............................

(Mostly by himself or with people)...

(People say)..................................... (Self-conscious—stare at him)...................................

....

(Trust people)... (Afraid of them)...

(Get along with wife) (or parents)............................ (Separated)...............................

(Run around).............................. (Wife (or husband) run around)...............................

(Sex with wife).. (First sexual exp.).......................................

(Steady girl)... (Expect to marry)....................................

(Type of girl go out with)..

(Sex with boys)... (Ever approached)...

(How often masturbate)................................... (What think of it)..................................

(Whom does he remind you of)...

(Like to be like him)..

Patient's Self-appraisal

(Worst part of body)... (Best part)...

(What's good about you).................................... (Bad about you)...................................

the statements he made may refer to himself as well as the figure. When used for diagnostic or therapeutic purposes, the associations may be extended and adapted to problems specific to the individual. The subject is also asked to explain features of the drawing that are not clearly identifiable. The information contained in these associations is of enormous clinical value. It will be systematized and discussed at greater length in future publications.

PART II

PRINCIPLES OF INTERPRETATION

INTERPRETATION

While the concepts underlying the technique of drawing analysis were developed more or less independently in
the course of studying thousands of drawings in clinical
contexts, their formulation owes much to established projective methods of personality analysis and to psycho-
analytical theory. Though some of the assumptions may
lack experimental verification, they have proved clinically
valid. The principles in the main were guided by study
of the clinical types in which the graphic trait in question
received emphasis. The file of drawings previously referred to, annotated in detail in regard to clinical and personal history, was used as a source for studying the meanings of particular graphic features. Although women and
children were included, circumstances of the writer's more
recent clinical duties facilitated the collection of sets of
drawings from more males over sixteen who were studied
for adjustment and emotional difficulties, than from any
other group. A considerable number of these sets of
drawings are combined with individual Rorschach pro-
tocols on the same subject, providing data for future
studies in relating the two methods. It is not intended to
convey the impression that the drawing traits selected for
discussion exhaust all possible angles of consideration by
any means. New aspects and features of the drawings
are being added constantly in an effort to refine the
method. Such features are pressing continually into view
in the course of coordinating individual case records with
drawings.

Again we repeat the basic assumption, verified repeatedly in clinical experience, that the human figure drawn
by an individual who is directed to "draw a person" relates
intimately to the impulses, anxieties, conflicts, and compensations characteristic of that individual. In some sense,
the figure drawn *is* the person, and the paper corresponds
to the environment. This may be a crude formulation,
but serves well as a working hypothesis. The process of
drawing the human figure is for the subject, whether he
realizes it or not, a problem not only in graphic skill, but
one of projecting himself in all of the body meanings and
attitudes that have come to be represented in his body
image. Consequently, the drawing analyst should feel free
to extract from the graphic product what the subject has
put into it. He should feel free to interpret directly aspects
which, with striking literalness, often reflect real life problems and behavior of the individual who is drawing. The
figure is, in a way, an introduction to the individual who
is drawing. Thus, when a subject erases his arms and
changes the position of them several times, it may be literally interpreted that the subject does not know what to
do with his arms in his behavior. If the fist is clenched,
he may literally be expressing his belligerence. If the eye
of the figure has a pensive, furtive, or bewildered (See
Figure 6m) gaze, it may often be characteristic of the individual who is projecting.

The size of the figure, where it is placed on the sheet,
the rapidity of graphic movement, the pressure, the solidity
and variability of line used, the succession of parts drawn,
the stance, the use of background or grounding effects,
the extension of the arms toward the body or away from
it, the spontaneity or rigidity, whether the figure is drawn

profile or front view are all pertinent aspects of the subject's self-presentation. In analysis, consideration is also given to the proportions of each part of the body, the tendency to incompletions, the amount of detailing and the area of concentration of detail, the amount and focus of reinforcements, of erasures and line changes, the degree of symmetry, treatment of midline, and above all, the mood expressed in the face or in the postural tone of the figure. Male and female figures of a set of drawings are compared in all of these characteristics.

Content, involving details of body and clothing treatment, is interpreted in terms of the functional significance attached to it. The functional and experiential values of such details have been checked with subjects capable of introspection and association on a conscious level, and with psychotic subjects whose unconscious thoughts emerged on a surface level. To validate further the basic functional criteria of interpretations of drawings, a comprehensive questionnaire is being prepared concerning the stereotyped meanings associated with specific body types, with certain types of features of clothing, and with such body details as a large nose, large feet, thick neck, jutting chin, broad shoulders, thin lips, large hands, as well as many other features of the human figure.

THE HEAD

Functionally, what can the head mean for the subject who is drawing a "person"? The head is the important center for the location of "self." Heads generally receive emphasis except in drawings of neurotic, depressed or socially withdrawn individuals. The head is essentially the center for intellectual power, social dominance, and control of body impulses. It is the only part of the body which is consistently exposed to view, thus being involved in the function of social relationships. Subjects have frequently verified this functional interpretation of the head when asked to give the best part of the body in their association to a figure, and further asked to explain why they consider it the best part. The obsessive-compulsive will frequently give an almost ape-like presentation of physical power in the figure he draws, while underplaying the head. In this instance, the head is definitely considered to be the organ responsible for his conflict concerning free expression of his impulses.

Disproportionately large heads will often be given by individuals suffering from organic brain disease, those who have been subjected to brain surgery, and those who have been preoccupied with headaches or other special head sensitivity. It may be considered that weakening of intellectual power and control fixates consciousness of the head as the primary organ in the hierarchy of body values. Although it may be argued that in cases of organic brain damage the large head treatment may be due to poor spatial judgment on the basis of intellectual defect, the fact that the head, in preference to other parts of the body, is emphasized must be seen in light of the functional value attributed to the head.

Since disproportionately large heads are a common feature in drawings, it would be profitable to examine the different psychological dispositions of individuals drawing large heads. The youngster whose emotional and social adjustments have been dislocated because of a severe reading or other subject disability will frequently draw a large head in his figure (See Figure 4m). The associations to the figure will most often give verbal corroboration of the importance that the youngster places upon education and intellectual attainment, and the frustration that he has suffered in that sphere. The mental defective will, for similar reasons, often give a large head. Frustrated intellectual aspirations, however, do not appear as readily in the associations to the figures drawn by the defective as they do in those of the subject disability of normal intelligence. The paranoid, narcissistic, intellectually righteous, and vain individual may draw a large head as an expression of his inflated ego. Another type of subject in whom disproportionately large head treatment is found is the inadequate male who gives the female figure, usually related to a mother-image, a much larger head than the figure of the male. In differential treatment between the male and female figure of the same set of drawings, the sex given the proportionately larger head is the sex that is accorded more intellect and social authority.

Young children constitute the largest group of subjects drawing large heads. The body is often given such meager emphasis in their drawing projections, that it is not clear from the functional standpoint if the smallness of the body or the largeness of the head is of primary significance. Functional analysis of the role of the head in the consciousness of the young child suggests that, because of a child's dependence, more social emphasis in terms of interpersonal relationships is involved, than the concentration of ego activity reflected in the meaning of the head in drawings of a more mature child or of an adult. It is not altogether clear why a young child of three or four will often draw a large head, perhaps with appendages issuing from it, as a completed representation of a person. It may be speculated that since locomotion and manual exploration of the environment (and of the child's own body) are important features of a child's early development, the appearance of legs and arms in drawings before the body, is functionally comprehensible. Since the ego development of a child, the sense of self in terms of intellectual power and control, is only in the nascent stage, we must examine the functional emphasis on the head from another angle. A child will offer a head as a completed person, but will never give an isolated trunk, neck, arms, or legs as representing a full person. Does the head loom large because it is the center of awareness in respect to feeding, sensory stimulations, and speech activity, or does it gain special significance from the fact that the most animated part of the social environment is the head of adults? It is with the head that surrounding adults smile, approve, frown, or scold. The head of the adult is the most important organ relating to the emotional security of the child. Perhaps the large head that dependent male adults give to the female figure in their drawings represents an emotional fixation on a supporting mother-image similar to that experienced by the child as a normal phase in its development.

Goodenough (17) has observed significant differences between the drawings that were obtained from boys and those obtained from girls, though both were instructed to draw a man. These differences deserve consideration from the functional standpoint. Girls are said to draw larger heads, shorter arms, smaller hands, shorter legs, and smaller feet than boys do (See Figure 4m). This difference in treatment may be related to the respective experiences of growing boys and growing girls in our culture. While girls have only to be pretty and decorative to command social attention, boys are expected to make rapid strides in development of physical and sexual power, in proficiency in athletics, to reach out into the environment more vigorously and to show more tangible accomplishment. It has been observed by many clinicians that emotional difficulties, behavior disorders, and scholastic problems occur more frequently in boys than in girls. More is expected of a boy. Competition with the formidable accomplishment of a father-image tends, in boys, to lead to discouragement, anxiety, and even retreat to mother protection, precipitating problems which girls are, in large measure, spared.

SOCIAL FEATURES — PARTS OF THE FACE

The face is the most expressive part of the body. It is the most important center of communication. The head or face is the most readily accepted, subjectively easiest to draw, and is, in the crudest drawings, often the most skilled part of the drawing. Subjects of all ages frequently offer the face (or head) as a completed drawing of a person, whereas, the trunk or any other part of the figure is, by itself, never considered a representation of a person. Subjects who draw the head as the last feature of their figure usually show disturbance in interpersonal relationships. The face may be regarded as the social feature of the drawing. The subject who deliberately omits facial features in a drawing showing careful and often aggressive delineation of contour and detail of other parts of the figure, is one who is evasive about the frictional character of his interpersonal relationships. This treatment is a graphic expression of avoidance of the problem. Superficiality, caution, and hostility may characterize the social contacts of such an individual. Omission of facial features has been encountered in "normal" subjects. Withdrawn and timid individuals will often dim out the facial features significantly, while emphasizing the contour of the head (importance of the "self" and a strong drive to social participation, but egocentrically blocked). We find, on the other hand, overemphasis and reinforcement of facial features by subjects who have, in their fantasy, compensated for their inadequacy and weakness of self-assertion by a self-image of an aggressive and socially dominant individual. This treatment is usually seen in profile and in combination with a dim line throughout the balance of the figure.

One deeply maladjusted adolescent drew a large head, replete with strong fantasy content and symbolic expressions of sexual vitality (a tremendously large, heavily shaded hat, excessively thick, heavily shaded lips, and much emphasis on hair). The head was almost separated from the body of the figure. It was out of line with the body axis, and looked like the head of a clay figure that was stuck on after it had fallen off. The subject indicated in his associations that the male figure was very bright, and though a Negro of poor circumstances, was aiming to become a doctor (large head for intellect and over-elaborated features in head for fantasy). The rest of the figure was significantly dressed in a dandy "zoot suit" with striped pants and pointed shoes, strongly suggesting the uninhibited expression of a strong impulse life. The subject is clinically quite two individuals in regard to the superficial, flashy, overactive and uninhibited expression of his immediate needs, on the one hand, and, on the other hand, the absorbed fantasy life which he nurtures privately, and which made the drawing task a really creative and cathartic experience for him.

Facial Expression

Facial expression has proved to be one of the characteristics of drawings which may be judged directly with considerable confidence. Individual judges will differ as to the exact description of a facial expression in a drawing, but in the experience of the writer, unanimity of judgment has been more the rule than the exception. Regardless of skill, we find that the subject will unconsciously set a tone to his drawing by an expression of hate, fear, bewilderment, aggression, rebelliousness, placation, meekness, or even of inappropriate affect. Yet if one were directed to draw a bewildered or happy person, he might not be able to do so. Experiments in projection of particular facial expressions upon specific direction and also in the course of specific moods induced hypnotically are being planned. A combination of drawing features seen frequently in schizoid subjects is the facial expression reflecting autistic and narcissistic preoccupation, with large size and aborted or blocked, movement trends to reinforce the fantasy quality of the subject's ego concentration. In these aborted movement figures, the fantasy impulse to movement is compelling, but the figure remains trapped in the axis of his own narcissism and exhibitionism, resulting most often in a static pose, which contrasts significantly with the evidence of internal movement.

The great variety of graphic treatment accorded the individual features of the face furnishes one of the main sources of content analysis. Introspections gathered from

individual subjects concerning their drawing habits, indicate the preponderance of fixed preference for specific
ways of making the mouth, the eyes, nose, and all the
features of the face. This would suggest that the particular
style selected to represent the various features refers stably
to basic personality characteristics. This hypothesis is being
checked with a study of constancy in drawing traits.

When extra lines are added to give grooving or special
expressive meaning to the face, other evidences of highly
developed intra-psychic elaboration are usually present in
the drawing. The lines most frequently indicated are in
the area of the naso-labial fold and on the forehead. Emphasis of this type is intended to add depth and maturity
to the face. Special reinforcement or a conspicuous bulge
of the forehead (seen in profile) is generally associated in
the subject's mind with intellectual capacity. The marked
occipital bulge that is sometimes seen in drawings may
have a similar meaning.

The Mouth

The mouth appears in children's drawings almost as
early as the head itself. This is entirely consistent with
the functional aspects of the child's growth. The mouth,
like the other facial features, shows a wide range of drawing projection. Emphasis upon the mouth may be expressed
by omission, reinforcement, special size, special shape, shading, erasure, or displacement. Oral emphasis is marked in
the drawings of young children, primitive, regressed, alcoholic and depressed individuals. Since the mouth is often
the source of sensual and erotic satisfaction, it features
conspicuously in the drawings of individuals with sexual
difficulties. Over-emphasis of the mouth is frequently

tied up with food fadism and gastric symptoms, profane language, and temper tantrums. Mouth detailing with teeth showing, in an adult drawing, is considered an index of infantile, oral aggression (See Figures 3m and 3f) and is often seen in drawings of simple schizophrenics or flat hysterical types. Children and low grade defectives will give this treatment frequently, but, unlike that treatment in schizophrenics, the oral aggression that is implied is more developmental than regressive in nature. Occasionally, even the tongue is indicated, intensifying the oral concentration on a primitive level. This also adds an erotic note.

The concave or orally receptive mouth is frequently encountered in the drawings of infantile, dependent individuals whose dependence is often also manifest in undue emphasis on buttons. Functionally, this type of mouth is primarily passive and is open to receive nourishment. It is an expression of oral dependence usually associated with demanding and parasitic adults. In young children the concave mouth is usually drawn in a front view. From a graphic and developmental standpoint, it is more normal than in adults. At the other extreme, we find the mouth that is represented graphically by a heavy line slash which, in the very act of drawing, communicates aggression. This treatment has often been correctly associated with the verbally aggressive, over-critical, and sometimes sadistic personality. A variation of this line is seen when the individual starts out with considerable pressure, but withdraws from the page rapidly, so that a heavy but brief mouth indication results. Interpretation of this treatment would follow that the impulse toward verbal aggression is strong, but the anticipated rebuff makes the individual withdraw cautiously. The single line for a mouth has been seen in profile drawings with a marked expression of tension, as if shutting the mouth tightly against something. This has been specifically seen in drawings of individuals who have had active fellatio experience. A not unsimiliar treatment, but with less tense line, was found in a patient who had lost his speech following an operation on his larynx. In this connection, it would be fruitful to study the mouth treatment of stammerers and those suffering from other types of speech defects. The wide, upturned line for a mouth, giving the effect of a grinning clown, is seen frequently in children's drawings and other infantile representations of the human figure. It has been interpreted as forced congeniality, an effort to win approval, or even inappropriate affect, depending upon other aspects of the drawing. In a drawing obtained recently from a pathologically depressed patient, the omission of the mouth was consistent with patient's expressed guilt about his oral aggression which was tied up in his mind with sadistic trends—a formulation that coincides with psychoanalytic theory of depression. Asthmatics may often omit the mouth.

The Lips

The detailing of lips when they appear in a drawing often sets the tone of the facial expression. Full lips, given to the male figure, are regarded as an effeminacy indicator (See Figure 6m). They most often appear with other features reflecting foppish and narcissistic interests. Sometimes the lips are developed with an especially sensual line and may be so interpreted. In rare cases, the lips have been specifically constructed to resemble the phallus, and these individuals have had actual sexual experience with the mouth. The lip treatment, just as other features of

the male figure, will often differ markedly from that of
the female of the set. This differential treatment will be
discussed in a later section. The elaborate, cupid-bow lips
in combination with other heavily cosmetized features in
the figure, are seen in drawings of the sexually precocious
girl. Whether the strong sexual drive is expressed in behavior must be judged from other aspects of the drawing.
An irrelevant line stuck in between the lips in the manner
of a straw or a toothpick has appeared in drawings of
individuals with a history of special oral erotism in their
sexual dispositions. The more crude and specific erotic
concentration on the lips or mouth is seen in drawings of
very immature individuals, and the drawings themselves
are crude. The more sophisticated treatment of oral-erotic
emphasis is usually accomplished by the inclusion of a
conspicuous cigarette or pipe.

The Chin

The chin, which is relatively insignificant in the consideration of facial beauty, and in actual life is just differentiated as a weak chin or a strong chin, receives quite
frequent conflict emphasis in drawings. The chin's importance in the body image stems more from its symbolic
significance as a social stereotype than from any concrete
functional role. In profile, the chin will frequently be
erased, reinforced, show a change of line, or made to jut
out prominently. Such treatment may be regarded as a
compensation for weakness, indecision, and fear of responsibility. It is interpreted as indicating a strong drive
to be socially forceful and dominant. Often this drive is
expressed more fully in the reinforcement of the whole
facial profile, in contrast to light lines elsewhere. In such

cases, the drive is usually not externalized in behavior, but is nurtured in fantasy. In full view, a break in line or heavy reinforcement may mark the emphasis of the chin. Frequently, the chin of the female figure is treated quite differently from that of the male figure. For instance, dependent males often symbolize projection of greater power onto the female not only in drawing a larger female figure, but in according it a much more prominent chin.

The Eyes

A considerable part of the function of social communication that is attributed to the head is concentrated in the eyes of an individual. The eye has not only been regarded as the "window of the soul," revealing the inner life of an individual, but it is a basic organ for contact with the outside world. "Seeing is believing" is only one of the numerous sayings which testify to the central function of the eye in accepting or rejecting the world about one. An individual who becomes deaf retains active contact with the environment, if only in an irritable and paranoid manner. He fights back. With some notable exceptions, the individual who is blinded loses contact with the world, is unable to fight back, because he is physically thrown at the mercy of the environment. He either withdraws, or becomes extremely dependent. The eyes are the chief point of concentration for the feeling of "self" and the vulnerability of the self. The common expression "to knock the living daylights out of you" suggests that one kills a person by depriving him of the use of his eyes. The eyes serve further to warn the individual of menacing and threatening elements in his environment. This is the function that the paranoid individual, who gives much graphic emphasis to the eyes, probably stresses most. The paranoid is over-alert to every detail about him. Ideas of reference may issue out of the fear of how people are reacting to one's own hostility toward them and the eye features centrally in that type of sensitivity. Individuals will sometimes draw a furtive and suspicious eye conveying ideas of reference. We also see the "piercing" eye in drawings, which appears to have more the function of an aggressive social tool than of esthetic or more comprehensive visual experience. (See Figure 3f.) The eye may also signify evil, power, or hypnotic control and in these roles is regarded as an intimate representative of the brain. When a person is "cockeyed" about something, he is confused in his thinking. Our emotional life and sense of security involve the eyes, insofar as we experience approval or rejection through the eyes of others. Literature has often placed much of the burden of a character study on description of the eyes of a person. The eyes rank high in the hierarchy of values of physical beauty and sexual stimulation. The eye is a complex organ from which our greatest pleasures and knowledge are derived.

The graphic treatment of the eye varies perhaps as much as its function. We see the large, dark, accentuated, or menacing eye creating an image of hostility and suspicion projected by the paranoid individual. Generally, girls make larger and more elaborated eyes than boys. Functionally, the eyes of a female may have more value for social adaptation and sexual stimulation. Also, females are usually socially more outgoing than males. The homosexually inclined male, often very extraverted in his social personality, may give large eyes with lashes to the figure of the male, in combination with a well specified high heel.

In other cases, the orbit area of the eye, indicated by a line, may be large, but the actual eye may be very tiny. These individuals may show strong visual curiosity, but have some guilt connected with that function, perhaps in the nature of voyeuristic conflict. The small eye appears often with other graphic indices of self-absorption. We find other subjects drawing a figure with the eyes closed as if to deliberately shut out the world in order to better concentrate on their own body narcissism. A less voluntary and more subtle projection of "not seeing," is the omission of the pupil and drawing only the outline of the eye. In this treatment, the world is not actively shut out, but it is perceived vaguely, as a sort of undifferentiated mass of stimulations with little discrimination of detail. (See Figures 4m and 4f). The unseeing eye is often symptomatic of emotional immaturity and egocentricity. Occasionally, this "empty eye" treatment is carried to the extreme of repeating small circles for the eyes, nose, mouth, and buttons on a figure. This treatment has been observed in extremely childish or regressed adults, low grade defectives, and sometimes in young children, perhaps as a reflection of dependence, shallow emotionality, and lack of discrimination. In one case of a female patient, the omission of one eye in the male figure was admittedly associated with sadistic fantasies of annihilating a rival brother by gouging out one of his eyes with her knitting needle.

The Eyebrow

The significance of the eyebrow has not been fully understood. There have been some individuals who gave special emphasis to the eyebrow, but adequate associations were not obtained from them. The brow interest probably shares the significance of other hair indications. The trim eyebrow, like the trim coiffure, is one of the social stereotypes reflecting refinement and grooming, while the bushy brow suggests more primitive, gruff, and uninhibited personality characteristics. The trim eyebrow carries the inflection of a critical attitude toward anyone indulging in free expression, as in the "raised eyebrow" associated with disdain, haughtiness, or query.

The Ear

The ear is frequently singled out for special conflict treatment. Viewed functionally, the ear is a relatively passive organ. It is not in full view in face-to-face contact, and is often hidden in the hair arrangements of the female. When the ear is exposed, women wear earrings more to distract from the ear than to call attention to it. Earrings serve to extend and decorate the contour of the face. Unless an ear is markedly outstanding because of size or special defect, it is of little esthetic interest. Ears are notoriously neglected in regard to cleanliness, and it is considered as vulgar to pick at the ears as at the nose. The inclusion of the ear in drawings is stabilized at a later age than the other facial features. It is thus considered less significant if a subject omits the ears in drawing the human figure, than if he omits a more active part of the body.

If the ear is made outstanding either by size, reinforcement, transparency through hair, shape, placement, or erasures, it may be assumed to have been particularly sensitized in the psyche of the individual who is drawing. This sensitivity may range from mild reactivity to criticism or social opinion to active auditory hallucinations, the degree of distortion of the ear often correlating with the intensity of the auditory experience that it reflects. Special ear attention in drawings may also be accorded on the basis of deafness, a consideration which is not frequently involved in an unselected group. The paranoid individual, with his guardedness, suspicions, and distrust most often gives ear emphasis, but the treatment is more modified than that given by patients who are, or have in the past, been disturbed by auditory hallucinations (See Figure 3m). The schizoid individual, with vague ideas of reference, often gives graphic notice to that symptom by moderate ear emphasis (See Figure 2m). One schizophrenic adolescent who gave a very skilled drawing of a man, which did not contain too many pathological features, was diagnosed on "blind" study of his drawing because of the unusual ear treatment. The ear was very large, had lines radiating from the center, and was excessively shaded. In the Rorschach, he had, it was later discovered, identified the whole Card III as an ear: "The black could be the inside, just the shadows in the ear, and the red could be the light shining on it." Often the homosexually conflicted individual will project ideas of reference and paranoid reactions in specific ear emphasis. The individual who is quick to take offense and is resistive to authority may show moderate ear accentuation on that basis. One mental defective, who was called a jackass among other names, and was very reactive to his unpopularity, managed to give his drawings the conspicuous ears of a jackass.

The Hair

Hair emphasis, whether it occurs on the head, on the chest, as a beard, or a mustache, is generally considered an indication of virility strivings. Emphasis may be expressed in the relatively large space given the hair (See Figure 8f), in the elaboration of coiffure (See Figure 2f), or in the vigor of shading that is accorded the hair (See Figure 6f). The symbolic significance of hair as an indication of sexual virility is traditionally confirmed by folklore and fashions. The classic story of Samson and Delilah need only to be mentioned in this connection. One has frequently observed the excitement with which the early adolescent greets the appearance of pubertal hair. In common parlance, something that is potent "will grow hair on your chest." It is common practice for the immature individual to grow a mustache or a beard in an effort to impress others with his maturity, despite the fact that the growth arouses suspicion of a disguised weakness of the face. The sideburns that some adolescents regard as stylish and manly, while they serve only to elaborate the "dandy" characteristics of their male figure, are associated with the "wolf" tradition in the mind of the person drawing.

Fashion for female hair-styles adds its testimony, especially as it is associated with specific characters. We have only to compare the prim, severe, and barren hair-do of the traditional spinster with the emphasis on abundance and freedom that is suggested by the hair arrangements associated with the sexually attractive and active female. Associations obtained from male subjects (usually adolescents or young adults) who give their female figure profuse and messy hair while giving the male figure a careful and precise coiffure, lead readily to the meaning of sexual disorderliness in connection with messy hair (See Figure 1f[1], *bottom*). To paraphrase the statements of many patients, "Her messy hair means she's untidy, loose and diseased."

(Projected immorality and syphilophobia often seen in the psychosexually infantile male.) A hairy woman is often regarded as sexually passionate. This differential treatment of hair between the male and female figure is generally seen in psychosexually immature males who are themselves narcissistic and are hostile to the female (See Figures 6m and 6f).

Emphasis upon wavy, glamorous, cascading hair, when combined with other outstanding cosmetic details, is seen in drawings of sexually delinquent girls or those who entertain glamour aspirations. This treatment is most commonly encountered in adolescence, but it is not uncommon in socially or sexually precocious children. Jewelry and other adornment details are often contained in such drawings. The vigorous shading of hair, with poor form delineation, is often an expression of the virility conflict brimming over into some sexually deviant behavior. Hair indications on the jaw have appeared in a few drawings of adolescents whose virility conflicts have taken on a schizoid caste. In one case, an acute onset of schizophrenic excitement, involving reiterated castration fears, was precipitated in the barber shop where his hair was being cut. Combinations occur wherein the female figure is drawn with hair conspicuously emphasized while the male figure, like as not in the nude, is topped with an incongruous hat. The diagnostic implication is of a regressed or schizoid character who has remained infantile sexually while nurturing vivid fantasies of virility. In the sets of drawings showing this type of differential treatment of the hair and the hat it is usually the female figure that is represented as the stronger individual of the pair. The symbolic significance of these hat-hair combinations in drawings of the regressed is not clear. Perhaps the hat serves to make the man presentable by concealing his impotence and in this sense represents an unconscious sexual compensation. It is interesting that the reverse treatment, that is, the hair for the man, and the hat for the woman, occurs very infrequently.

The Nose

The nose is considered in drawings to have essentially the sexual symbolism with which it has been traditionally invested. The nose, like the penis, is in the midline of the body and protrudes from it and displacement from below to above is not uncommon. Most male subjects give considerable attention to the nose both in graphic treatment and in verbal description of the figure drawn. Adolescents very often regard the nose as the worst part of their body. Frequently, a history is given of an adolescent who refuses to leave his room for months, because of sensitivity about his nose. One young male schizophrenic, who had committed a sadistic sexual murder, complained of the embarrassment about some imagined defect on his nose which had persisted through adolescence. This preoccupation was definitely related to masturbation guilt. In the drawing of another patient, the mouth displaced the nose. This substitution was especially significant because the patient involved was arrested for performing cunnilingus on children. In his sexual behavior his penis had actually been displaced by the mouth, and, in the drawing, a mouth was drawn in the place where the nose (penis symbol) should have been. Many other clinical instances of having frankly regarded the nose as a penis symbol were obtained in the course of drawing analysis. The social stereotype of a long nose suggesting sexual virility and a "button" nose being childish is reflected in frequent anecdote.

Since a majority of the patients one encounters in a mental hospital or clinic population have sexual difficulties, either of immaturity, feelings of inferiority, of impotence, or homosexuality, the prevalence of nose emphasis in drawings is quite marked. In profile, the nose may be reinforced, enlarged or made smaller, erased, shaded, crossed out, or made conspicuously long. In full view, the nose may be shaded, reinforced, or omitted. This conflict treatment of the nose may be given to both figures of the set of drawings. At other times, the subject accords this type of conflict treatment to the figure of opposite sex. The way in which the subject distributes his own traits between the male and female figures may derive from the pattern of his sexual identifications. It is also of interest to note that often the omission of the nose in one figure will be paralleled by over-emphasis of the nose in the other figure of a set. Impotence in the older male is often symbolically indicated in the drawing of an excessively long nose, while the sexually uncertain or inadequate adolescent is more likely to project his sexual difficulties more frequently in a display symbol like the tie, a conspicuous fly on the trousers, or a shading or cutting off of the nose. It is tentatively considered that the shaded or cut-off nose relates more to castration fears for auto-erotic indulgence (See Figure 6m), while the reinforced nose is suggestive of a more direct compensation for inadequate sexuality. This observation will bear further checking. If the *nostrils* are indicated with any degree of emphasis, they are regarded as a specific accent on aggression, an interpretation which is generally sustained by other features of the drawing studied.

THE NECK

The neck is often singled out for graphic emphasis by individuals who are disturbed about the incoordination of their impulses and their mental control functions. There is some consciousness of a split in their personalities. Conflict in regard to the strength of the super-ego is suggested. Structurally, the neck is the link between the body (impulse life) and head (intellectual, rational control). From the esthetic standpoint, the neck, like the ears, receives little attention unless it is especially deformed. Primitive people select that area for elaborate adornment. The more royal the caste of the person, the more conspicuous and elaborate the neckgear to emphasize the separation of the head from the body. It is of interest that religious symbols and charms are worn around the neck, rather than around the wrists or ankles. Royalty and cultured, "stiff-necked," rigid, and over-moral persons who are distinguished for their vaunted mastery over their impulses, are associated with a tall thin neck, while the short-necked, pyknic individual is associated with gruffness, bull-headedness and behavior that is more guided by impulse than by intellect. Adornment of the neck with jewelry and frills is more designed to distract attention from the neck proper and focus it upon the bosom line or contours of the face. Occasionally, a specific and irrelevant horizontal line, cutting off the head at the neck, appears which subjects are unable to explain. A more subtle way of accomplishing this severance is suggested by the appearance of a tight choker necklace in the female figure which is otherwise unelaborated as to clothing (See Figure 7f).

Conflict treatment of the neck implying incoordination between impulse and rational control appears in many drawings, since the balance between self-expression and restrictions imposed by society is especially precarious in a complex and contradictory cultural milieu. The neck is often given as the most important part of the body by subjects when they associate to the drawings. One subject explained its importance in terms of its being the locus of the Adam's apple. One paranoid individual stated that without the neck, "you could not turn your head to see who was after you or what was doing about you." The globus-hystericus lump in the throat gives further evidence of selection of the neck as a focus of conflict. The more serious efforts at suicide aim at the neck. Several psychotic patients with guilt in regard to earlier fellatio experiences, showed symptoms of extreme neck discomfort. One child who was about to be tested, looked up at examiner mutely and indicated that he had just had a tonsillectomy. It was soon discovered that the child had undergone a circumcision in connection with excessive masturbation, and that the symbolic castration was readily referred to the neck. Although the drawing of the neck does not require any special skill, it is one of the later parts to enter the drawings of children. The omission of the neck is seen as a factor of immaturity in drawings of children, adult defectives and regressed individuals. Capacity to deal rationally with, and coordinate impulse with adjustive behavior is indeed lacking in these individuals.

The long and often very thin neck, resulting in a striking separation between the body and the head, is most often seen in the schizoid, or even schizophrenic individual. Clinically, many of these individuals suffer from a sense of body weakness which they express in a compensatory drive for physical power and aggression. In their verbal associations they regard the chest or shoulders as the best part of their male figures and deplore the functions of the head. They are physically inferior and psycho-sexually infantile and a number of this group have been referred for study because of their compensatory acts of aggression. The excessively long neck on one figure of a set may often be combined with the absence of a neck, or a very stubby neck on the other figure of the pair.

Adam's Apple

The Adam's apple appears in drawings with comparative infrequency. It has been seen mostly in the drawings of young males as an expression of a strong virility or masculinity drive. Special interest in the Adam's apple has been restricted to the sexually weak individual who shows little differentiation between male and female characteristics and is uncertain about his own role. It has occasionally been given the female (virility assigned to her). Patients who were asked about their knowledge of the function of the Adam's apple related it to swallowing food, and were not sure if females as well as males had it. Nevertheless, they seem to use it unconsciously as a masculinity indicator.

CONTACT FEATURES

We build our image of "self" out of our impulses, our behavior, and the reality about us, and the representation of the body image in drawings tends to invite the graphic expression of any conflict which might be experienced in any of these spheres. The body image changes with mental and physical disease, with frustrations and alterations in adjustment. The organization of the whole body model develops slowly with the enrichment and interiorization of experience. The universally more skilled and detailed treatment of the head, relative to the body, in the drawings of young children and in drawings of deteriorated individuals, tends to confirm the slowness with which the body image is built up and the vulnerability of it in the face of mental disease, conflict, or personality disorganization. Movement and contact with the outside world unite the body image. Individuals who, because of physical or mental disease are restricted in movement or contact with the outside world and are left to feed largely on the perceptions and sensations derived from their own body, may either project an elaborate expression of inner fantasy activity, or lacking active fantasy compensations, may portray an empty, vegetative, regressed, and sometimes silly figure, reducing the image of the personality to the barest and crudest essentials. In general, it may be said that movement as an expression of fantasy in drawings tends to diminish with age as does the actual behavioral mobility of an individual. Children and young adults, more than others, show movement in their drawings— both actual functional movement and the aborted movement pertaining to fantasy elaborations. They will also be more naturally attracted to the projection of social-hero stereotypes.

Various graphic indices of weak contact with the outside world and increasing withdrawal into the body axis are seen in the maladjusted. Some degree of somatic concentration, intensified narcissism, and weakening of contact features appears in most drawings of neurotic or psychotic individuals. Such drawings will often combine infantility with active fantasy in the form of well developed detailing in the area of the body, but arms do not leave the body, eyes look inward, and the mouth frequently will be a concave, receptive one. Much of the life and animation of the figure may be dependent upon perfection of attire with complete absence of flexibility. The frozen and aborted movement where the intention toward movement is clear, but the figure is trapped in self-contemplation, falls into the "weak contact" group of drawings.

Arms and Hands

Considered functionally, the arms and hands are weighted with psychological meanings referring primarily to ego development and social adaptation. It is with the arms and hands that we feed, dress, perform skills, explore our body and contact persons about us. It is with the arms that we love and caress, hurt and kill, disrupt and adapt. Considering these far-reaching implications of the role of the arms and hands, it is no wonder that so many subjects express difficulty in the projection of them in drawings. The most commonly omitted feature is the hands, with the feet following as a close second. If the hands are drawn, they may often fade into vagueness or be dimmed out (lack of confidence in social contact, in productivity, or both). They may be shaded vigorously—suggesting guilt in regard to aggressive impulses or masturbatory activity. They may be put behind the back in an evasive manner. This is seen frequently in female figures of young girls with glamour aspirations who bite their nails. The figure is often dressed in an evening gown, with hands behind the back. The hand may be put in the pocket, a treatment seen most often in delinquent or psychopathic young adult males as an expression of evasiveness. In associations, hands-in-pockets is connected with masturbation, with being a loafer, perhaps with holding on to a gun. Occasionally, the hands are drawn quite large by young boys as an expression of strength. Excessive size indicates compensation for weakness or reaction to some guilty use of the hands.

In determining the contact of the individual with the environment, the direction of the arm placement is considered important. Do the arms extend away from the body towards the environment? Do they hang limply at the sides of the figure? Do they press closely and tensely towards the figure (See Figure 6m), or do they venture out bravely, only to return to the body axis? Interpretations of these various treatments must be related to other features in the drawing studied such as indications of the degree of narcissism, of withdrawal, of self-display or vanity, or of tension. In general, the direction and fluency of the arm lines relate to the degree and spontaneity of extension into the environment. Arms that are extended in a horizontal, mechanical fashion at right angles from the body line cannot, however, be considered a true extension into the environment. This treatment is usually in connection with simple and regressed drawings and refer more to shallow and affectless contact than they do to fluid interplay with the environment. Not infrequently, the direction and tonus of the arm treatment give the flavor and mood of the figure.

The arms may be drawn in single dimension, or they may be otherwise frail or wasted, indicating deficit and weakness either as a physical reality or psychic reaction. In individuals who have functionally reduced the effectiveness of their arms either by force of circumstance or by self-incapacitation, the arm structure is usually indicated, though in a deficit treatment. Omission of arms can never be considered as a casual oversight. Arms enter childrens' drawings very early. The reactions to drawings by many subjects attest to the fact that arms are always in active awareness, if only to arouse complaint that they are difficult to draw. Schizophrenic or extremely depressed subjects may omit the arms as indication of positive withdrawal from people and things. On rare occasions, a subject may omit the arms on the psychogenic basis of guilt. Occasionally the arms of the female figure may be omitted. This treatment has been seen only in adult males who have felt rejected by their mothers and, in turn, have felt alienated from and unacceptable to contemporary females in their environment. The arms of the male figure in such cases may be reaching out, overextended (See Figures 3m and 3f). An asthmatic child who was seeking the affection of his mother by making excessive demands upon her, drew abnormally long arms, though the arms were in single dimension, wavy-lined, and had no strength in them. This treatment was graphically unlike any other part of the drawing. Special reinforcements or indications of interest in muscles of the arm are usually seen in combination with other features of physical-power strivings such as chest and broad-shoulder emphasis. The very long arm has been associated with ambition either for accomplishment or for acquisition, depending upon other aspects of the drawing. The "freezing" of the hand at the genital region is most frequently associated with individuals preoccupied with auto-erotic practices. This placement is sometimes rationalized as an indication of swinging the arms in walking.

Fingers

Fingers are extremely important in the experiential pattern of a person. They are the real contact points so that, for example, the prints of the fingers, rather than any other stable part of the body are used for identification. Fingers are so important as to be individually named. They feature in basic counting. They stand out as projections that are usually exposed to view. They are flexible and the tools of manipulation. They carry the potentialities for aggression (the trigger finger, putting a finger on somebody, or putting one's finger in the pie). Fingers are used in communication by mutes and are involved in much symbol language to ward off evil, or bless (keep one's fingers crossed, V for victory, and other examples). Fingers are also used in various orifices of the body to comfort or titillate, and in that connection they may be involved in the generation of guilt.

The significance of fingers in the functional economy of the body cannot be overstressed. Fingers, as a rule, enter children's drawings before the hands do. In an adult, the drawing of fingers without benefit of the hands is regarded as a mark of infantile aggression. Such fingers are most frequently drawn in single dimension, with heavy pressure, and in combination with other regressed and primitive features in the drawing. The petal or grape-like formation of fingers, short and rounded, though normal for children, when seen in adult drawings, are usually associated with the clinical traits of poor manual skill and infantility. Severely shaded or reinforced fingers are generally regarded as guilt indicators. In the cases that have been collected, the guilt has referred mainly to stealing and masturbatory activity. The speared or talon-like fingers have been seen with paranoid features in drawings to support the suggestion of overt aggression. (See Figure 3m). The clenched fist, especially with the arm away from the body has occurred chiefly in drawings of adolescent delinquents whose rebelliousness is fairly close to surface behavior. When the clenched fist is pressed tautly towards the body, the significance lies more in the direction of inner and repressed rebellion that finds expression in symptoms rather than behavior. A mitten type of hand and finger development has been associated also with repressed aggression, but it is more evasive and non-committal in character, tending to be associated more with furtive outbursts of aggression than with somatic symptomatology. The hand with the fingers carefully articulated, but hemmed in by a line, cutting off their contact possibilities, is interpreted as another expression of repressed aggression (See Figure 2m). It is seen in individuals who incline to withdraw from emotional contacts for fear of their aggressive impulses becoming overt. Occasionally one sees abnormally long fingers as a conspicuous feature in regressed drawings (See Figure 3m). These have been in conjunction with shallow, flat, and simple types of personality development in adults who have not used their fingers for vocational or social adaptation. The exact meaning of these fingers is not clear, since they often are not associated with openly aggressive personalities, but the possibility that it may have a sexually symbolic significance is consistent with other features of the drawing. Ambitious and aggressive individuals with acquisitive dispositions may draw more than five fingers on a hand. This is not uncommon in childrens' drawings. Fingers that are drawn with joints and nails carefully indicated (See Figure 3m) are interpreted as indicating obsessive control of aggression on the part of the subject. Another expression of aggression is seen in the fingers that are formed like a claw, or a mechanical tool. In drawings of individuals preoccupied with masturbation, the index finger or thumb may be given conspicuous or rigid treatment, or the dismemberment (castration) of a significant finger may be shown.

Legs and Feet

It has already been mentioned that legs, and especially feet are sources of conflict and difficulty in many drawings. Examining these parts of the body for their functional significance, we may understand why insecurity of footing, literally interpreted, is shown in most problem drawings. In addition to the potentiality for contact, which the legs and feet share with the arms and hands, they bear the added responsibility of supporting and balancing the body proper and of making possible locomotion of the body. The bed-ridden, depressed, discouraged, or psychically withdrawn individual may show resistance to drawing feet and even legs, and may sometimes compromise by giving a seated figure. In some cases, such individuals may project a compensatory trend toward movement and activity in their drawings, which can be judged from other aspects of the drawing (especially over-perfection) to be largely of a fantasy character. Frequently, a subject who is acutely disturbed sexually, may refuse to complete the drawing below the waistline, or just indicate a few representative lines for that section of the body. A less drastic shock reaction is seen in the mechanical, heavy line of demarcation at the waistline in drawings where it could only be a weak excuse for a belt as an item of clothing. Occasionally, the reluctance to deal with the legs and crotch area by psycho-sexually immature males is handled by drawing the outer contours of the legs (in front view), making a sort of skirt outline, and then drawing a line in the middle to divide this skirt-like figure into trouser legs.

Full bodies with tiny, wasted, thin, shaky, or shaded legs are seen in drawings of the involutional or senile individual as an expression of feelings of decline or deficit. In adult male drawings showing other graphic evidence of sexual disturbance, shading of the legs, or delineation of legs (usually two-dimensional) through transparent pants (See Figure 3m) adds evidence of homosexual panic.

The legs of females, unlike those of males, are usually exposed and have acquired specifically sexual significance. They feature frequently in the associations to the female figure drawn as the best or worst part of the body, and often receive conflict treatment in the form of erasures, reinforcement, or change in line. The narcissistic and psycho-sexually immature male will often give a kindly representation of the male and a hostile, hussy figure of the female with characteristically twisted leg perspective, so that one cannot tell whether it is the front or rear of the figure. The legs in these cases will be quite masculine and muscular. It is assumed that this type of treatment has some sexual significance involving the confusion of sexual characteristics.

The *foot* features more conspicuously in the male figure than in the female. Feet drawn with all-but-deliberate fidelity to phallic likeness may be offered by individuals who give other drawing indices of sexual inadequacy and preoccupation. This treatment of the feet, as well as the symbolically eloquent drawing of an excessively long nose, occurs more frequently in drawings of males who have turned their thirty-five year mark, than of younger males. The foot may be given special attention by erasures, lengthening, shortening, change of line, or shading. Sexual symbolism of the foot has been verified repeatedly in the associations given to such drawings, in literature pertaining to sexual aberrations, and in popular anecdote. It seems likely that this sexual significance may apply as well to the fact that girls tend to draw small feet while boys as a rule draw relatively large feet. This differential graphic treatment of the foot appears to refer as well to problems of general security of footing in the environment. The foot appears as well to have aggressive implications arising out of its function in propelling and leading the body forward and as an instrument of attack.

Toes

When toes are indicated in a figure that is not intended to be a nude, they are regarded as an accent on aggressiveness that is almost pathological in nature. Toes, unlike fingers, are seldom exposed except in sandals or bathing slippers, and normally they do not appear in the drawing of a clothed figure. In keeping with the interpretative significance accorded the display of toes in drawings, the recent female trend of painting toe-nails and exposing them in open-toed shoes may be regarded as an expression of increased feminine aggression. It is certainly viewed as such by the more conservative. As with the encasement of fingers, the confinement of the toes shown in a drawing behind a line joining their distal ends is considered to indicate a blunting or repression of aggressive trends.

MISCELLANEOUS BODY FEATURES
The Trunk

The trunk is often limited to a simple oblong, a square box or a circular unit. The round figure has been associated with less aggressive, more undeveloped, and more feminine drawings, while the figure involving angles is considered more masculine, corresponding with principles of expressive movement that pertain to all creative projections. The trunk is occasionally omitted. The attachment of appendages to the head with omission of the trunk has already been noted in connection with the drawings of very young children, the particular significance being referred to the developmental stage of maturity. In adults, the trunk is seldom omitted. Patients with involutional and sclerotic involvement on occasion fail to give the male figure a trunk, while shading the trunk of the female figure anxiously (rejection of own body and aggression against the female). In culturally restricted individuals the corresponding clinical traits were rigidity and narcissism. Occasionally, the trunk is identified on the basis of its position in the figure rather than on the basis of definite graphic delineation. In such cases the trunk is simply designated

as the upper part of two parallel lines running in an unbroken continuity from the head to the feet. The figure
is thus left devoid of any enclosure to represent the trunk
and is consequently without any substantial body what-
ever. These drawings are usually small and seen in regressed, primitive, or disorganized individuals. Another
type of treatment is seen in the reluctance to close the
bottom of the trunk in drawings where some bottom is
given. This is interpreted as indicating sexual preoccupation. Occasionally the closing is effected by a separate
connecting line indicating disturbance surrounding that
area.

The specially thin body as a representation of the self-
sex is usually indicative of some discontent with the body
type possessed by the individual who is drawing. It may
be a direct representation of body frailty or weakness, or
it may suggest a compensation for unwelcome rotundity.
In one case, a very slender figure represented the subject's
fear of becoming stout. She had associated body fullness
with maturity and her central problem revolved about her
resistance to growing into adulthood. Another child of
ten, who was markedly undersized, vividly fantasied the
feeling of growing as he drew two parallel lines close together from the bottom to the top of the page to indicate
a tall body. A double or confused body contour, especially in drawings of females with glamour fantasies, will
often spot a preoccupation with weight, particularly in a
context of oral emphasis in the drawing.

Breasts

The most consistent and significant interest in breast
treatment is noted in the drawings of emotionally and

psycho-sexually immature males. The breasts are erased, shaded, returned to frequently for some additional furtive lines to mark preoccupation with that part of the figure (See Figure 8f). Occasionally, the breasts are obviously evaded and converted into carefully drawn pockets in the breast area. In several drawings, the breasts were actually showing through the pockets, when no other transparency occurred in the drawing. Whether the breast is given a low, pendant line, suggesting that the figure is a mother-image representation, or whether it is given the high, firm line of a youthful female figure is significant. The accentuated bosom is usually in the context of a strong and dominant mother-image, in drawings of both male and female subjects (See Figures 8m and 8f). The female who gives large breasts and pelvic development to her figure may be regarded as strongly identified with a productive and dominant mother-image, almost in a matriarchal sense. One young adolescent who envied her mother's breast maturity, drew a low breast line with an especially heavy brooch to contain the supposedly large breasts. Another late-adolescent who feared maturity, featured a tiny, budding breast line as of a pre-adolescent figure, in her drawing of an adult female figure. One adult neurotic who was acutely disturbed about his furtive sexual interest in his youngish step-mother and who was given to immature sex practices drew a breast in profile with obvious indication of marked conflict. He erased and redrew the figure of the breast many times, altering it in size and shape, until finally it stood out from the body like an erect phallus. As he surveyed the product of his assiduous efforts he was impelled to remark gloomily, "H'm, it can't stand up by itself that way."

Shoulders

The width and massiveness of the shoulders are considered the most common graphic expression of physical power and perfection of physique. In male drawings, massive shoulders emphasized at the expense of other parts of the figure, are seen in adolescents and frequently in sexually ambivalent individuals as an overcompensation for feelings of body inadequacy. The female subject who draws the female figure with powerful shoulders (See Figures 7m and 7f) may be suspected of some degree of masculine protest if that interpretation is corroborated by stress on other features of the drawing which are related to virility. Men have commonly had padded shoulders in their tailoring. Women have adopted them more recently along with other traditionally masculine sartorial manifestations. The problem of physical inadequacy is so very often the tortured preoccupation of the emotionally disturbed male that conflicted uncertainty as to how broad the shoulders of the male image should be made occurs frequently. When the shoulders are marked by erasures, reinforcements, and uncertainties, it is safe to conclude that the drive for body development as an expression of masculinity is a basic preoccupation. In some drawings of male subjects presented either in front view or in profile, the effort to achieve broad shoulders in the male figure results significantly in the likeness of a bosom, while the female of the pair may be given broad shoulders clearly. This confusion of physical power and maternal symbol indicated in the male figure is usually combined with other features of sexual confusion in the drawing.

Hips and Buttocks

Both the hips and buttocks may receive undue attention in the drawings of the homosexually inclined or conflicted male. It is not uncommon to see the male figure twisted in perspective in order to focus an overdeveloped buttock. This may be seen in both nude and clothed figures, in profile and front views. Often the hip area will show confusion, a break or change of line, or particular widening, in conjunction with conspicuous treatment of the buttocks. This conflict in regard to the hips may be expressed more subtly in an accentuated horizontal flare of the bottom of a man's jacket, extending beyond the main body area, although the jacket is clearly buttoned. Whether the homosexual trends are made overt in behavior may sometimes be judged by the context of the drawing. In female figures drawn by females, an exaggerated hipline may be associated with the awareness of power that relates to the functional potentialities of ample pelvic development.

The Waistline

The waistline is sometimes given as the only representation of clothing on a figure. Specifically, it serves to zone the trunk of the body, separating the "above" from the "below." Viewed from a functional standpoint, this demarcation divides significantly differentiated areas of the body. In the male, the "above" is the chest area which embraces the primary body features of physical strength; i.e., chest expansion and body musculature. The "below" refers primarily to the area of sexual functioning, with the legs sharing the significance of sexual strength on a more symbolic level. Functionally, the "above" of the female is related to nutritional factors, being distinguished primarily for its breast development. It is the area most commonly emphasized by the orally dependent, mother-fixated male. The "below" in the female, refers mainly to sexual and reproductive functions, with the pelvic extension of the hips bearing more specifically upon the reproductive aspects. For better or worse, the legs of the female bear considerable responsibility for the total social impression of sexual allure. Adolescent girls, being at the threshold of adult sexuality, show the greatest amount of leg conflict.

Conflict at the waistline may receive expression in many ways and roughly accords with the intensity and handling of the conflict. Thus, sheer delay in drawing the waistline, combined with impatience to draw it on the companion figure of a set of drawings will result in opposite extremes of low and high waistlines, expressing blocking in regard to meeting the body area of sexuality. A reinforced waistline, or a broken line may serve to give notice of an irritable and fairly direct expression of tension in this problem of "zoning" the body. More control and rationalization of this tension may result in an elaborate belt, which shows the tendency of converting tension into esthetic and self-display forms. An excessively tightened waistline, giving a corseted and pent-up appearance, suggests precarious control which may find outlet in temperamental outbursts. On occasion, the three body zones, the head, the trunk, and the area from the waist down, are drawn out of line with each other. There is conveyed an indication of a chronic disturbance in the coordination of major dimensions of the body image pointing to an inadequacy in personality integration which is the more serious in that it involves disjunction among sexual drives, strivings for physical power and rational control.

Anatomy Indications

Clear anatomical indications of internal organs of the body are rarely encountered except in the drawings of schizophrenic or actively manic patients. The suspicion of somatic delusions which is aroused by such graphic treatment is usually justified. A more moderate type of somatic consciousness may be expressed by the meaningful placement of a few sketchy lines in the chest or pelvic region. Indications of rib lines are also not essentially pathological, since they serve to give the appearance of physical power. The inclusion of sexual organs in a drawing offered in response to the instruction, "draw a person," is seldom seen in any but the drawings of professional art students, persons in analysis, and schizophrenics. Delineation of body parts through transparent clothing is a different matter from the drawing of internal organs. In the former case the body is usually drawn first and the subsequently added clothing simply fails to conceal it. It is not a positive drawing-in of the organs. Such transparencies are most frequently seen as legs showing through trousers in the male figure (frequently shaded and indicative of homosexual panic), or as the contours of the female body showing through the skirt (most commonly associated with furtive sexual fantasies or acts of a deviated character in male subjects who are vastly preoccupied with infantile sexual impulses). The latter treatment was seen chiefly in drawings by male subjects with involutional sex problems.

Joints

Unless a person draws a "peanut man," as a stylistic evasion of meeting the body problem, he seldom indicates the elbow, shoulder, knee-joints, or knuckles in his drawing (See Figure 3m). Individuals who indicate the joints may be suspected of a faulty and uncertain sense of body integrity. Joints give a "strung together" quality to a figure, a mechanical and artificial note which brings into question the smooth, dynamic functioning and stable organization of the body image. The schizoid, the frankly schizophrenic individual, and occasionally the body narcissist in decline will lean on joint emphasis in order to stave off feelings of body disorganization. Indication of joints may also be seen in drawings involving static, fantasy movement. Most drawings that involve joint emphasis are in a setting of mother dependence, psycho-sexual immaturity, and are paired with a female that is more aggressive, larger, and more dominant than the male figure.

CLOTHING

The body image can be extended, altered, and enhanced by clothing. A large surface of our bodies is usually clothed. Disregarding the individual theories in regard to the function of clothing, it is generally accepted that clothes have always had some libidinal significance. Clothing is to some extent a compromise between modesty and blunt body display in all circumstances except where it is definitely required for protection. Most subjects tend to evade the problem of whether to clothe or not to clothe a figure they have drawn. The majority compromise with a crude, vague, or token indication of clothing. If a person makes a preliminary inquiry as to whether he should draw a figure with or without clothes, it may be assumed that he is troubled by a strong body self-consciousness. The embarrassment with which the question is asked and the clinical data relating to the individual case tend to justify this interpretation. Not infrequently the identity of the person projected, even when the projection is un-conscious, may be inferred from the character of the clothing. Thus, street attire on the female which reaches to the ankles may be judged as indicating that the figure represents a mother image (See Figure 5f). Some male subjects draw clothes on a young figure consistent with the mode appropriate to the prime of the father, thus suggesting strong identification with the father.

Study of drawings in coordination with clinical his-tories reveals a small, but significant proportion of indi-viduals who consistently overclothe or underclothe the figures they draw with a great deal of conviction and energy spilled into the drawing task. For purposes of convenience, those who overclothe the figure may be referred to as clothes-narcissists, and those who under-clothe the figure as body-narcissists. Although both of these groups share in common infantile and egocentric emotionality and more than the average degree of sexual maladjustment, they do offer interesting contrasts in their drawings, and correspondingly, in their personalities. The clothes-narcissists use clothing essentially as a means of social and sexual enticement. The body exhibitionism and self-display are accomplished by decoration while the body proper is underplayed. The body-narcissist, however, if he is a male, will most often draw a frank display of muscle development with concession to clothing given only in the form of a pair of brief athletic trunks (See Figure 2m). The drawings of the male clothes-narcissist, on the other hand, most often resemble a fashion-plate, with draped suit, highly padded shoulders, handkerchief carefully arranged in breast pocket, and other details of perfect tailoring and grooming. Interestingly enough, the female of the pair may be given a bathing suit with more muscle than seductive allure. The female figure of the body-narcissist on the other hand, is often fully clothed, but in such manner as to emphasize the sexual features of the clothing (See Figures 2m and 2f).

These contrasting types of clothing treatment parallel significant differences in personality. The clothes-narcissist is superficially quite sociable and extraverted. The sociability is, however, more motivated by a strong appetite for social approval and dominance, than by a genuine object interest. Drawings of self-sex done by females of the clothes-narcissist type are characterized by over-attention to cosmetic features, adornment, and glamour. In general, these individuals veer toward a psychopathic type of adjustment. The body-narcissist, with his display of muscle power, accords more with the schizoid, self-absorbed, and introverted type of personality. He is preoccupied with his body processes, often to the point of engaging in long and strenuous periods of body development for its own sake. Sexually, he probably restricts himself largely to auto-erotic stimulations. He derives no genuine satisfaction in social intercourse, preferring his own fantasy ruminations.

Conspicuous Buttons

Button emphasis in terms of shading, exceptional pressure, or odd or irrelevant placement on the figure, occurs especially in dependent, infantile, and inadequate persons. It is seen more in male drawings than in female drawings, and more in children, especially boys, than in adults. In emotionally regressed adults, a mechanical and not too relevant row of buttons drawn compulsively down the middle of the figure, perhaps in combination with an incongruous hat, tends to suffice for the representation of clothing. Sometimes buttons serve to elaborate a strong midline emphasis, reflecting egocentric and somatic preoccupation. Occasionally, a large and emphatic button is placed at the umbilical point of a figure with no other indications of clothing.

Because buttons appear on so many drawings of maladjusted individuals, it would be profitable to speculate on the functional and symbolic meaning of buttons from various angles. The fact that a button often virtually in the shape of a round buckle is sometimes placed at the umbilical point, and the fact that button emphasis occurs mainly in drawings of mother-attached individuals, leads to the suggestion that the psychological significance of buttons may be connected with the umbilical symbol of mother-dependence. The umbilicus is the center of the body and important things generate from the center. It is the most arresting physiognomic aspect of the abdomen, and may, on the basis of its appearance be associated with the nipples. For the infant, the nipple has the magic quality of being all-sustaining, requiring little effort on his part.

It is this association with nutritive function that lends plausibility to the interpretation of dependency.

Buttons are a conspicuous feature of uniforms, and are especially abundant on uniforms of bell-hops and cadets, thus suggesting some relationship to the authority-submission complex (See Figure 3m). This reinforces the dependency meaning from another angle. Authority and control, with their corollaries of submission and dependence are involved in many common sayings about buttons. Thus, to push a button is to master some person or thing by remote control. When everything is buttoned up, it is under control. Considered functionally, buttons are opened to expose the body and closed to conceal it, and in this respect reflect body consciousness. Buttons on cuffs add an obsessive note to the dependency feature.

Pockets

Like buttons, irrelevant emphasis upon pockets is seen in drawings of infantile and dependent individuals, and more in male than in female subjects. Empirically, special pocket treatment has been associated more specifically with affectional or material deprivation as background for psychopathic adjustment (See Figures 4m and 4f). Adolescent boys arrested for purse-snatching, often include special pockets in their drawings or give an accessory pocket-book to the female, thus offering graphic evidence of the frequently neurotic and symbolic nature of the offense. Associations of subjects to the meaning of pockets describe pockets as a place to keep private possessions, as offering concealment for.gun or for masturbatory activity. One patient who drew a figure with hands in pocket remarked, "I always got that bad habit. My mother said that a fellar who keeps his hands in his pockets will never amount to anything." To a growing boy, a large pocket full of all sorts of gadgets is a symbol of ego-expansion and maturity. Pockets may thus be used by adolescents as an expression of virility strivings which conflict with emotional dependence upon the mother. Females seldom indicate pockets in their drawings. They are inclined to be more independent, and their clothing, except for a shirt-waist dress or a masculine tailored suit, seldom has pockets.

The Tie

The tie is a common sexual symbol, seen mostly in the drawings of boys and young male adults (See Figure 4m). On the other hand, in males over forty, conflict over sexual inadequacy tends to be expressed, graphically, in an egregious lengthening of the nose or in excessive attention to, or other type of incongruous treatment of this organ or of the foot. The last touch that a young man puts on his appearance when he goes out on a date is the straightening of the tie and perhaps the perking up of his breast-pocket handkerchief. Emphasis of both the tie and hand-kerchief theme is common in drawings of sexually inade-quate males. Effeminate and dandyish men are known for their collection of flashy ties. Homosexuals are said to wave their ties to attract attention. In drawings, ties vary from the uncertain, tiny, and debilitated-looking tie of the individual who is despairingly aware of his weak sexuality, to the long and conspicuous tie, sometimes deco-rated with phallic-like details, of the sexually aggressive individual who is driven to excessive compensation by fear of impotence. Relatively few bow-ties are indicated in drawings collected by the writer, and possible relationships with clinical data could not therefore be explored. Occasionally, the tie is drawn as if it were flying away from the body. This has been seen in cases of overt sexual aggression, and usually indicates intense sexual preoccupation. In passing, it may be noted that the black or white bow-tie is generally worn on formal, restrained and conservative occasions, while the gay bow-tie is worn on occasions that call for a touch of youthfulness and irresponsibility.

The Shoe and the Hat

Symbolic phallic investment of the shoe, expressed graphically in unmistakably suggestive designing, and in conflict treatment involving erasures, alterations, shading, or change of line, appears most commonly in the involutional male subject who is suffering from some degree of impotence. Not infrequently, the shoe receives special attention in the elaboration of eyelets, laces, or bows, with a precision of delineation not characteristic of the rest of the drawing. It is most frequently seen in drawings of men done by pubescent girls and seems to represent an accent on obsessiveness which, in its focus on an article of clothing often symbolically sexual, may be associated with sexual impulses. The obsessive detailing of the shoe appears to be a distinctly feminine characteristic in graphic expression.

When the hat appears on a figure in the absence of other clothing, other features of regression are found in the drawing. The hats are often handled in such a manner as to confirm the phallic significance which is attributed to hats in psychoanalytic investigations. In one case, convicted of indecent exposure, the brim of the hat, in profile view, was drawn so that its extensions beyond the crown bore a striking resemblance to an erect phallus. The hat may often be especially decorated, conspicuously large, or it may have the hair or forehead showing through it. The latter type of transparency usually occurs in the context of a generally primitive and unelaborated treatment of the figure as a whole and is quite often found to be symptomatic of primitive sexual behavior in the subject. The hat is almost never given both the male and female figures of a pair. The female figure usually gets the abundant hair, and the male figure, the hat.

Other *sexual symbols* most commonly encountered in drawings are the pipe, cigarette, gun and, less frequently, the cane. The pipe and cigarette are seen mostly in drawings of young male adults or adolescents. The gun most frequently enters the drawings of young ·pre-adolescent or adolescent boys, while the cane is seldom seen in subjects below forty. The symbolism of the pipe, cigarette, and gun is too obvious to need discussion. When they are made inordinately large, conspicuous, or smoking actively, they usually denote sexual preoccupation so acute as to be actively disturbing the subject. This interpretation does not apply to the drawings of young boys who elaborate a dramatic shooting theme. One patient, who had perpetrated a murderous sexual assault upon his own fiancee, drew the hat of the male figure first, followed by a cursory indication of profile. Immediately he stuck a pipe into the mouth before proceeding with the rest of the drawing. The pipe was very large, reinforced, and actively smoking. When the patient was asked if the male figure was married, he replied "He would have to be, to be smoking a pipe that way." The cane enters drawings of persons in middle or later life who are reluctant to accept decline. It is rarely found in drawings of younger people. In a group of drawings obtained from displaced European professionals, of about involutional age, the cane featured rather significantly. Occasionally a large brief case is drawn over the sexual area of the figure in pretentious display, indicating an effort to substitute intellectual power for inadequate sexual power.* Emphasis upon the fly of the trousers is seen in individuals preoccupied with masturbation, unless, as in the case of football pants, the fly is, in actuality, an essential and conspicuous part of the kind of trousers represented.

STRUCTURAL AND FORMAL ASPECTS

Thus far, the principles underlying the projection of the body model have referred primarily to the content of the drawing of a human figure. The formal aspects are, however, of equal significance for diagnosis and analysis. Some types of drawings are so limited in content as to place the whole burden of analysis upon the structural features. These structural features involve a variety and refinement of detail, much of which is being submitted to experimental verification. For the purposes of this introductory survey, only brief consideration of some of the major factors will be attempted.

---

* The following dream, reported by a patient in therapy, who was presenting severe sexual difficulties, is illustrative of the symbolic uses of briefcase and shoes: "I am walking in the street and I am going to see someone. I suddenly looked down on my clothes and saw that I was dressed in pajamas. I then stepped into a store to buy a briefcase. The man did not have the kind I wanted. I was looking for a briefcase, barefoot, while my shoes were being fixed by the shoemaker in the same store." The patient is extremely verbal, intellectualizes all of his problems, and has enormous exhibitionistic drives.

Theme

When an individual is asked to draw a "person" does he project an anonymous figure that takes shape with his associations to it? Is the figure a stereotype, a specific person, or an avowed self-image? Individuals who are self-consciously trying to prove their sanity may label the figure drawn as that of an "average" or "normal" person. If a character stereotype is selected, such as a soldier, a cowboy, a policeman, or a gangster, it may be safe to assume that some degree of self-identification is involved on a fantasy level. This assumption of self-identification applies equally to children who draw Superman or Dick Tracy though the stereotype is a socially prevalent one and does not have as intense individual significance for the boy as for the adult. It has been noted that the returning veteran, especially if he has had some difficulty in adjusting himself in the service, frequently will draw a soldier or sailor with obvious self-identification. In these instances, the female figure of the set does not depict a stereotype. The soldier or sailor that is drawn is usually large and contains other indices of fantasy development. It is likely that these individuals were motivated in their incentive to join the armed forces by fantasies too narcissistic and unreal to sustain their subsequent adjustment. If a snow-man, peanut-man, or line drawing is offered as a serious representation of a "person," an evasion of body problems is indicated. These figures will often be smaller and more to the introversive (left) side of the page than the subject's fuller representation, perhaps because of the tension involved in "putting something over." In the case of a patient indicted for murder, the snow-man proved upon association to be a symbol of the precarious control that the subject had over his own body integrity. The patient felt, like the snowman, artificially sustained, and tended to dissolve under the heat of pressure. This patient was subject to psychotic outbursts into which periodically he gained some insight. Another significant treatment is the projection of a figure which in all of its graphic characteristics is markedly younger or older than the subject. If the self-sex is younger, some emotional fixation at that age or a wish to return to youth may be assumed (See Figures 7f and 8m). If the figure is older, an identification with the parent-image (of self-sex) may be indicated.

Action or Movement

In terms of action or movement rather than the person portrayed, a variety of themes appears in drawings. The figure may be posing, walking, in combat, giving something to somebody, orating, or greeting somebody. The majority of drawings obtained from an adult hospital, or clinic population, are static or at best portray a person who is "taking a walk." Action is more common in the drawings of pre-adolescent boys. Girls show a marked preference for figures on display. When highly developed action is intended, action which does not bear relevantly upon the subject's age, IQ, vocation, or appropriate interests, fantasy preoccupation may be assumed. Whether the fantasy is of a constructive or pathological nature must be judged from other aspects of the drawing. The fact that action and fantasy are more common in boys' drawings checks with the observation that girls are considered more realistic, practical, and oriented to social requirements, while boys entertain fantasies of power and adventure. The drawing that conveys a clear impulse to movement, but is blocked and counteracted by static, autistic, or introversive features (See Figure 2m) is seen primarily in schizoid or schizophrenic individuals whose strivings toward accomplishment and power are strong but entirely fantasy-bound.

Succession

The sequence of procedure of a drawing is important. It is the one aspect which cannot be judged unless notes are made while the subject is drawing. Most people fall within normal and logical limits in their procedure. Some, however, work in confusion, scattering over the drawing planlessly. This may be due to an impulse disorder, manic excitement, or schizophrenic thinking. The over-cautious, compulsive individual often develops each tiny area bilaterally, in a stimulus-bound fashion, fearful of venturing into the general contours of a goal idea (See Figures 6m and 6f). Subjects starting with facial features. and then enclosing them, those starting with the hat instead of the head, those drawing the head as the last feature of the drawing, and those starting with the feet and working upwards are all giving expression to some measure of interpersonal maladjustment involving reluctance or incapacity to undertake emotional commitments (See Figures 5m and 5f). Occasionally, an individual will interrupt the drawing to give extra emphasis to some particular area of conflict and may even return to that area several times while he is drawing. Hesitation to proceed beyond the head or beneath the waistline indicates reluctance to face conflicts relating to those areas.

Symmetry

The construction of the human figure is essentially symmetrical. Elementary art instruction stresses that approach, and yet few individuals, trained or untrained, give undue stress to bilateral detailing. Extreme symmetry produces rigid effects. Rigidity in the figure often appears correlated with corresponding postural states in the subject which, from the psychosomatic viewpoint, may be considered a hypertonic muscular defense against the release of repressed emotional states on the one hand, and, on the other hand, as a protection against a menacing environment. Marked symmetry may produce mechanical, formalistic, and even bizarre effects as in the drawings of the paranoid schizophrenic. Occasionally, a subject starts his drawing with the sketch of an armature or with measurement details (See Figure 6m). Such props are used for bilateral control by individuals who fear body imbalance, who may suffer some degree of depersonalization, or who may experience a compulsive drive to control the unruly and spontaneous impulses which threaten the integrity of the self. Perfectionism and an impulse toward exhibitionism are correlated features contained in such drawings. Individuals giving over-symmetrical drawings are usually compulsive, emotionally cold and distant, and precariously controlled personalities (See Figure 2m). It is of interest to note that the organs, such as the heart, stomach, brain, neck, and the penis, which feature most in the somatic disturbances of the emotionally conflicted individual, are not strictly bilateral. In the compulsive character, this absence of bilaterality may tend to threaten or disturb the integrity and balance of the body and thus produces symptoms.

Marked disturbance in symmetry may be seen in drawings of neurotics as an expression of body awkwardness, a sense of incoordination, or general physical inadequacy. The figure may actually appear lopsided in a manner which, curiously enough, often faithfully reflects the subject's own appearance. The largest group in which irregularity of symmetry is noted consists of those suffering from confusion of lateral dominance, that is, the motor intergrades (See Figures 4m and 4f). These individuals are, in fact, awkward in their motor coordinations. In their figure drawings, one shoulder will often be conspicuously narrower than the other. The distance between chest and arm-pits may be markedly discrepant. Often the arms and legs differ markedly as to length, width, or both. The hypomanic or hysterical individual, those suffering from some impulse disturbance, in general those that have an excess of spontaneity, may show disturbances in symmetry, largely on the basis of carelessness, poor control, over-activity, and diffusion.

In considering the significance of departure from symmetry, it was necessary to determine which is the right and which is the left side of the figure, as intended by the subject who is doing the drawing. This problem has been investigated in various ways. For most subjects, the right and the left are oriented from the focus of the person being portrayed, rather than from that of the observer.

Midline

The problem of midline emphasis in drawings, although occasionally related to considerations of symmetry, usually plays a somewhat different role. The midline is essentially the body axis, and, as in the Rorschach test, may involve problems of an unconscious nature. The midline may be treated elaborately with Adam's apple, tie, buttons, buckle, and even a fly on the trousers (See Figure 6m), or it may be indicated by a vague, light line down the middle of the trunk. Somatic preoccupation, feelings of body inferiority, emotional immaturity, and mother dependence, feature in the clinical records of many of the individuals who stress the midline. The drawings of this group are somewhat conspicuous for their very aggressive female figures, and the emasculated, effeminate and collapsed male figures. The verbal associations usually conform with the graphic portrayals of the male and female figures. A row of irrelevant buttons will often constitute the midline emphasis. This treatment is frequently seen in schizoid or schizophrenic individuals whose physical inferiority and mother dependence are in the forefront. Infantile, narcissistic, older subjects who are approaching involutional decline and are unable to accept it may give crude emphasis to the midline of the figure, reflecting their somatic preoccupation.

Size and Placement

In general, interpretation of directional placement of the figure on the page is similar to that utilized by Mira in his Myokinetic method and by scientific graphology as well. If the figure projected on the page is toward the right, it is environment-oriented. Toward the left, it is self-oriented, high up on the page, it is related to optimism, low down on the page, it is related to depression. This rough classification of directional trends has aided clinical analysis. It is probable that the size and placement of a figure are less subject to conscious control and variability than other structural aspects of a drawing. The manic individual cannot help but scatter the figure over the page with an expansive use of paper and an extravagance of energy. An experiment involving the constancy of line, size and placement projection of the figure is in progress. The writer had occasion to examine a collection of diagrams of cell bodies copied by a high-school class of biology students exposed to the same sample. An effort was made to deduce personality traits of the individual pupils from the size, placement, line, detailing, and incompletions. The resulting observations checked well with the teacher's independent judgments of the personality traits under consideration.

The very large figure, placed aggressively in the middle of the page is seen most often in the grandiose paranoid individual who possesses a high fantasy self-esteem. This treatment is quite different from the paranoid conditions usually associated with chronic alcoholism, involutional changes, or senility. In these latter cases, the self-esteem is definitely not high and the figure is correspondingly small. The placement of the figure is relatively high on the page, and often gives the impression that the figure is adrift in space. Lack of insight, unjustified optimism, a low level of energy and, basically, a lack of secure footing are some of the psychological correlates of this type of projection. One patient, who could be summed up as an infantile, unstable, hypomanic schemer, filled the whole page with an idealized, pompous, narcissistic bust for a male figure, commenting spontaneously while he was working, "My father was an egocentric egomaniac." In reality, patient duplicated his father's overweaning narcissism. He was full of fads, schemes, and bluff. In associations to the drawing, he remarked, "Maybe I cannot associate with anyone but myself. I'm too self-centered."

Tiny figures may be seen in the regressed and vegetative schizophrenics as an expression of low energy level and a shrunken ego. In contrast with the relatively active facial features and positive line of the small figures drawn by the alcoholic, involutional, or senile individual, the drawings of the regressed schizophrenic are marked by simple and even primitive features with no modulation in line treatment. Micrographic figures are also encountered frequently in the deeply repressed and neurotically depressed individual. The figures in these instances are usually more detailed, and may encompass fragmented lines, frequent erasures, significant reinforcements, and considerable shading. The feet may be omitted altogether, or an extra line may be added for footing. In brief, areas of specific and active conflict are indicated in one form or another.

The large figure is not restricted to the overactive manic, the grandiose paranoid, and the fantasy inflated individual. The aggressive psychopath may well give a fairly large figure, but it may be shifted to the left or introversive side, corresponding with the felt inadequacy that is expressed in other drawing indices of insecurity. Large, empty, poorly proportioned, and weakly synthesized figures are often seen in the mentally deficient or organic case, reflecting the shallow emotionality, lack of insight, and poor reasoning powers characteristic of these individuals. The line is usually heavy and corresponds with other features of aggression in these drawings. The hysterical psychopath will not infrequently offer fairly large drawings, centrally placed, but the collapsed portrayal of the body, usually in combination with a relatively intact and detailed head, will serve to differentiate the hysteric from organic or defective types. In addition, the quality of the line is more simple and solid in the organic and defective.

Stance

The stance of a figure may be regarded in a similar light as the stance of a real person. Are the feet wide apart, placed with aplomb in the middle of the page? The assertiveness suggested by such stance is frequently counteracted by insecurity of footing expressed in tiny, pointed, shaded or reinforced feet, by a ground line, or by a hesitant and faint line throughout the drawing. The legs may be apart, but the figure is not planted firmly on the ground. The legs may float off into space, and the whole figure may be aslant, giving a definite impression of drifting, and precariousness of perch. This type of stance is quite common in older chronic alcoholics. A not too dissimilar type of figure representation may be seen in drawings of the hysterical psychopath, but with a significant difference in line. The line given by the hysterical psychopath fades in and out in regard to pressure, while the pressure of the jagged line of the alcoholic drawing is usually constant.

The stance that is marked by legs closely pressed together, especially when the figure is small, perhaps shaded, or otherwise reflects repression, is seen in the tense, self-conscious, awkward, and apprehensive type of neurotic. When this type of treatment is extreme in the female figure, it may, if the subject is a girl, suggest fear (or repressed wish?) of sexual attack. Its occurrence in the female figure of a male subject, suggests anticipation of resistance to the fantasied assault. One patient, convicted of impairing the morals of a minor, gave the male figure a wide stance, but drew his female, identified in his associations as his wife, with legs held tightly together. His chief complaint against his wife was her sexual rejection of him. The paranoid and schizoid individual may often give some version of the tight stance, in combination with arms pressed closely to the body as if to ward off the blows of the environment. Reserve and withdrawal may be judged from this type of treatment.

Perspective

In general, consistent profile treatment of a figure is interpreted as an index of evasiveness. Subjects explain their preference for profiles simply: "It's easiest. I don't have to draw the other half." Although profile figures suggest a fear of commitment, it is not to be assumed that accessibility and frankness are characteristic of all subjects who do a front view. Profiles are seen more frequently in drawings of boys and men than in those of girls and women. The impression that females are more sociable and superficially more accessible in clinical contact is confirmed by many observers. The full view also suggests a tendency to exhibitionism and display, which, in our culture is more characteristic of females. When male subjects give an overdressed figure in front view, exhibitionism may be suspected. Profiles are considered intellectually more mature, and are very rare in young children's drawings, not only because of the greater difficulty in handling profiles, but perhaps also because of the greater frankness of young children. Right-handed persons do profiles facing the left side of the page. Hands behind back or in pockets are considered a more direct and naive expression of evasiveness than profile treatment.

The profile head with the full-view body is commonly seen in boys, especially adolescents, and seldom encountered in girls' drawings. The resulting posture is a strained and unrealistic one. It is usually regarded as an indication of social uneasiness, some guilt in relation to social contacts, perhaps some degree of dishonesty, and yet with it all, a drive to exhibit one's body, which prevents the execution of a consistent profile. Occasionally, the head is drawn in profile, the trunk in front view, and the legs in profile. Any such rotation and distortion in perspective is interpreted literally as a sign of poor judgment and perspective in the subject. The most pathological handling of perspective in drawings is seen in the confusion of profile and full face in the elaboration of features of the head. Most commonly, the forehead and nose will be in profile and the eyes and mouth in front view. The eyes and mouth are more strictly orifices and have no projection value as the nose has, and perhaps are easier to handle in front view. Furthermore, the eyes and mouth are ontogenetically more infantile in the development of drawing skill. This confused type of treatment is encountered in primitive cultures. In the writer's collection, this confusion occurs in low grade defectives, in organic cases with schizoid underpinnings which have become accentuated, and, most frequently, in schizophrenic characters (See Figure 3m and 3f). The unschooled Southern Negro of dull intelligence who has been clinically known to show many distortions of perception (22) may offer such confusion of head treatment without being actually psychotic.

The male and female figures of a set of drawings are often given in different perspective. Many male subjects draw their own sex in profile, while drawing the female in front view. It seems probable that this discrepancy in treatment refers to a contrast of protectiveness in regard to exposure of one's own self and the readiness to expose the female figure. Female figures which clearly represent a mother-image, are usually drawn in full face, particularly in the case of adolescents and young adults, since this is most consistent with the habitual manner in which contact with one's own mother is experienced. These are the less certain areas of interpretation and require further investigation though they are not without support in clinical validation.

Type of Line

The pressure, the firmness, and the solidity of the line used in drawing are considered more basically characteristic than some of the other formal features. The line may be faint, dim, or heavy. It may be solid, broken, fragmented, or reinforced. It may be thin or have real dimensional thickness. The line of the contour of the body is essentially the wall between the body and the environment, and often reflects the degree of barrier, vulnerability, sensitivity, or insulation of the subject. Chronic schizoid alcoholics and those suffering from depersonalization fears, or from acute conflict in regard to withdrawal trends, may give a thick heavy line as a barrier between themselves and the environment. The body wall is built into a substantial structure as though to ward off the impact of the environment and to guard securely the contents of the body. The apprehensive neurotic individual occasionally draws heavy lines for much the same reason that the defective and the organic draws heavy lines. In such cases, the pencil is kept compulsively glued to the page in a virtually unbroken line, as though the subject derived support and reassurance from the contact. The actual contact with the paper in the course of constructing various aspects of the human figure appears, upon close observation, to be a very intense experience subjectively. Psychic interruptions, caused by conflicts aroused in special areas of the figure, are frequently expressed in a sudden change in line, or in a conspicuous gap.

The dim line occurs most frequently in the timid, self-effacing, and uncertain individual. The dim line is also frequently fragmented or sketched. Body contours may be uncertain and individual parts of the body blurred in outline. Often this dim line is contrasted with features of aggression contained in the drawing, producing the effect, interpretatively, of strongly aggressive impulses that are inhibited in social contact. In drawings in which the contour of the full-view head is heavy and reinforced, while the facial features are dimly sketched, the interpretation that a strong wish for social participation contrasts with shyness, timidity, and self-consciousness in actual social expression has proved clinically valid. Indicative less of neurotic trend and more of withdrawal and autistic realization of narcissistically oriented drive to social dominance, are those side-view drawings in which the line of the facial profile is heavy and emphatic while the lines of the balance of the usually large figure are dim and uncertain. The fading in and out of line, with spotty reinforcements, is commonly seen in the drawings of individuals given to hysterical, often specifically amnestic reactions to their difficulties. In these cases, the head and facial features may be well delineated, while the body is blurred and appendages fade away into random lines. The faint, "ectoplasmic" line is relatively rare, appearing mainly in withdrawn schizophrenics. The acutely excited schizophrenic or the manic, on the other hand, give very heavy lines as graphic expression of their excess of motor aggression. A fuzzy, broken, or tremulous line with light pressure is often seen in the schizoid alcoholic as distinguished from the heavy line used by the paranoid alcoholic.

CONFLICT INDICATORS

Differential treatment given to any area of the figure is considered significant of conflict relating to that area. Attention may be drawn to a particular feature of the drawing by a subtle break, dimming out or reinforcement of line, by erasures, or by shading. Conspicuous omission of hand, legs, or feet is important. The mouth may be omitted from the female figure of a male subject because the wife or mother scolds. The nose may be crossed off, or the hand may be specifically cut off from the arm with a line in a manner to suggest fear of castration. The eye may be large in outline, and yet no inside detail is given, though the drawing is otherwise carefully executed. There is usually good reason why the eye in this type of treatment is deprived of its function of seeing. Perhaps there is thus indicated an unperceiving, self-absorbed contact with the world, contrasting somewhat with the more active shutting out of the world suggested by the closed eye.

The parts of the body which receive conflict-indicating attention, most often through omission or special treatment are, in approximate order of frequency, the hands and feet, the shoulders, the arm, the nose, ears, crotch, and hip-line. Interpretation of the specific graphic treatment is based, in accordance with the general interpretative principles set forth in this discussion, upon the functional significance of the part stressed.

Erasures

This form of conflict treatment is mostly seen in neurotics, obsessive compulsive characters, and in psychopaths with neurotic conflicts. Young children, defectives, regressed schizophrenics, organics, seniles, manics, retarded depressions, and chronic alcoholics, unless of distinctly neurotic type, seldom erase. Erasures are considered an expression of anxiety, but differ from line reinforcement and shading, insofar as they show overt dissatisfaction. Motor restlessness is a common symptom of this group. Erasures are more subject to conscious control than the line-reinforcement or shading expression of conflict. They represent an attempt to alter and perfect. It is to be noted that erasures are unrelated to the objective difficulty of drawing the part which has been erased. They frequently result in deterioration of form rather than improvement, thus tending to confirm the interpretation that erasure means conflict. Pubertal girls erase profusely.

Shading

Any degree or type of shading is considered an expression of anxiety. As with other types of conflict projection, the particular area of the figure that is shaded is considered in the light of its functional significance. The vigorous, aggressive scribbling to cover up something must be seen as an expression of both discharge of aggression and of concealment. It is most frequently found in psychopaths and young children. The fun of repetitive movement may be involved in the case of children. It has been noted that sexually sadistic males often shade the sexual area of the female figure with considerable force. The indicated perverse urgency of sexual drive is emphasized not only in the restriction of the shading to the specific locus, but particularly in the fact that, in the case of clothed figures, the unconscious treatment of the skirt as though it were transparent indicates that the individual is subject to serious lapses of judgment especially with respect to his sexual behavior. Occasionally, this impulsive outburst of motor tensions is directed against the whole figure, usually of the subject's sex, in a manner suggesting violent rejection of the body. This is most often seen in subjects who are inferior either as to physique or health status.

The more frequent type of shading consists in the light, dim, and uncertain lines which furtively accent particular parts of the figure. The areas most often shaded in this manner are the chest in the male figure, indicating sensitivity to physical inferiority, and the breasts in the female figure done by the male subject, indicating conflict involving mother dependence. Female subjects may put a few subtle lines on the skirt, in the area of the genitals, suggesting furtive and inhibited sexual concern. Another type of shading may be described as patterned and stylized. In Rorschach terms, this treatment corresponds roughly to the use of maps and x-rays instead of clouds, with similar interpretative significance. The design serves to rationalize and so reduce shock with regard to the particular area of conflict. The shading of the boundaries of clothing may be associated with conflict in regard to body concealment. It may involve at once the impulse and the fear to expose the body. The body thus gets wrapped up neatly but emphatically with clothing boundaries.

DIFFERENTIAL TREATMENT OF MALE AND FEMALE FIGURES

The difference in technique and general treatment accorded the male and female figures drawn by the same subject is often remarkable. Since wide variations, unrelated to objective difficulty, are often observed in drawings made by one subject, the problem of skill in drawing, except as an IQ or talent index, is considered incidental.

It is not infrequent for an infantile, sexually immature male subject to draw a well modulated, detailed, and kindly representation of the male figure, perhaps in profile, while the female figure of the set, an obvious mother-image, is drawn in front view with virility and hostility constituting the dominant graphic features. When the subject shows grandiose, exhibitionist and self-inflation features, the female may be somewhat smaller in size, though the menacing female image is maintained. The smaller size, despite the greater force and dominance of the female figure, may indicate a belittling attitude toward the female in defense against the image of castrating authority assigned to her. It may, on the other hand, be an expression of the negative emphasis given any but his own space-filling figure. The female subject who is guided by strong masculine strivings may strengthen the woman and weaken the man of the pair (See Figures 7m and 7f). This may be accomplished by reducing the size, infantilizing the figure, or neglecting aggressive or contact features of the male figure.

The problem of projection of traits, both from a graphic standpoint and from the verbal associations to the drawings, is extremely challenging. The projection of self-traits of the subject and of his problems may be restricted to the figure of self-sex, it may spread over the male and female figure of a pair, or it may, to a large extent, be directed toward the figure of the opposite sex. Often, only the defects may be projected onto the opposite-sex figure. Subjects may describe the figure of one sex in terms more appropriate to the appearance of the figure of opposite sex, the verbal and graphic renditions of each being often at variance. Some subjects are so identified with the opposite sex that they are unable to draw their own sex image. The particular type of treatment, graphic and verbal, accorded the pair of figures drawn by a subject may be associated with the degree of identification with the male and female figure that is characteristic of the subject. From the standpoint of sexual identification, it is assumed to be most normal to draw the self-sex first. From an empirical point-of-view, it is of interest that evidence of some degree of sexual inversion was contained in records of all individuals who drew the opposite sex first in response to the instruction, "draw a person" (See Figure 6f). The drawings in such cases showed considerable sexual confusion. The greater the confusion and scrambling of sexual characteristics in the male and female figures of a pair, the greater the sexual maladjustment of the subject drawing the pair. Occasionally, one finds an identical description of the male and female figure given by individuals whose narcissism is so entrenched that they are unable to project any but their own traits and wishes. The attitudes of the subject toward the sexes is considered the basic determinant in the differential treatment.

DEVELOPMENTAL CONSIDERATIONS

The chronological age of the subject does not materially alter the interpretation of specific characteristics of his graphic expression since the latter is based on body image projection and the basic functional meaning of its parts. However, the particular significance of a drawing trait for a specific individual must be referred to the appearance of that trait in his age group so as to permit evaluation of the extent to which the trait is a "normal" expression of a developmental phase. As yet, no specific norms in terms of personality expression at various ages have been established. Enough is known about common drawing expressions of the child at various ages, however, and about developmental personality phases to give pertinent background. In studying the drawings of children at various ages, we find that stress is put on the aspects of the drawing which refer most intimately to the emotional needs, meaningful experiences, and problems of the maturing child.

Functionally considered, it is natural for a child of three or four to draw a person that looks more like a spider than a human being, that is, a sort of head with legs and arms attached to it. The social stimulations represented by the head, the locomotion interest expressed in the feet, and the manipulation and extension into the environment that are represented by the arms, are normal to the child's growth experience at that age. The trunk has, as yet, not entered the child's consciousness significantly as a differentiated and meaningful experience. It appears in drawings consistently later than the head and appendages. In an adult, this type of drawing would represent severe regression or mental retardation. To consider another example of developmental interpretation, a normal child's drawing may well be lacking in perspective and have numerous transparencies, since a child's thinking is specific and concrete. A child usually draws what it knows and not what it sees. Thus, a dress superimposed upon a body with transparency is common, or even hair showing through a hat. Similarly faulty perspective and transparencies in the drawing of an adult, however, are considered serious irregularities reflecting poor judgment, poor focusing of a problem, and weak discrimination of essentials. Perseveration, so common in children's drawings, may reflect in the child the sheer joy of repeating satisfying motor patterns, while in adult drawings, perseveration may indicate a low IQ, deterioration, or neurotic refuge in safe, routine, and confined areas of activity. We also find shading appearing frequently in childrens' drawings. Though the interpretative significance of shading as anxiety is retained, the meaning of a child's shading may relate to the general insecurity of a child in an adult world, rather than to individual pathology.

CONCLUDING REMARKS

The brief survey of principles of drawing analysis here presented is essentially preliminary and tentative. As far as they go, however, the interpretative principles and leads described have been reasonably verified in clinical application to the analysis of thousands of drawings studied in coordination with individual case records over a period of fifteen years. Numerous detailed personality studies involving the "blind" interpretation of drawings, have repeatedly validated the method. Most of the clinical observations and statements of specific meanings were arrived at as a result of careful study of all the different types of cases in which a particular drawing trait occurred, with special reference to the context in which that trait appeared. Enough is known covering the drawing expression of a number of clinically homogeneous groups to contribute substantially to differential diagnosis. Nevertheless, for the further codification of the method, it is necessary to study both the dynamics of the intra-individual pattern and the drawing characteristics common to particular clinical groups. At this stage of systematization, it is safest to focus on the psychological meanings of specific drawing traits, in the context of their inter-relation, rather than to attempt to set down rigid formulae for guidance in interpretation. The drawing of the human figure must be understood as an expression of moods and tensions, and as a vehicle for the individual's projection of his problems and his mode of experience-organization as reflected in his body scheme. As with all projective techniques which seek to grasp as a whole and yet analyze the complex pattern of personality organization, the technical psychological knowledge and the clinical sagacity of the analyst are indispensable to the translation of the language of the method into the traits and the behavioral dynamics and trends of the individual studied. Although "blind" analysis technique is necessary for experimental vertification of principles, and is frequently used by the writer, the clinical use of drawings as a diagnostic or therapeutic aid is most fruitful when the drawings are interpreted in light of all available case-history data.

Finally, although the drawing of a person is not expected to tell all invariably, it does, invariably tell something, and in many instances a great deal. Drawing analysis has the potentialities of becoming a refined instrument of personality investigation if accorded the research effort that it merits. Such is the richness of its psychological implications, that experience with the method must stimulate the formulation of innumerable problems and hypotheses of primary significance to the field of personality organization, expression, and projection. Drawing analysis is offered as a valuable supplementary clinical method. The time and material involved are economical and need no special preparation. Drawings can be done anywhere and at any time that a paper and pencil can be made available, and for this reason have been hopefully collected by many clinicians. With slight modification of administration, the method is quite adaptable to group application. There is no doubt that many of the formulations here offered will need to be changed in the light of future experience. Many details are in need of further exploration, validation, and refinement. There is broad room, indeed, for the extension of the method through discovery of new interpretative leads. What is important is that the basic orientation of the method as here presented offers a sound framework for such progress.

PART III

ILLUSTRATIVE CASE STUDIES

ILLUSTRATIONS

Although most drawings can be analyzed so as to afford a fairly comprehensive understanding of the personality structure, notes and interpretations on the drawings contained in this section are intended primarily to illustrate the specific application of some of the principles which have been set forth. Interpretations have been checked with more comprehensive case histories than are used for the brief case summary. They will be presented in a manner more suitable for didactic than literary purposes. A number of the cases are being presented here in a form similar to tabular itemization, with individual meanings being assigned to specific drawing features. This is not to be construed as sanction to deal atomistically with either the drawing traits or their interpretations. It must be borne in mind that the ultimate goal is the patterning of traits in context, to be reconstructed in terms of a whole personality. It is, however, recommended that initial attempts at personality analysis through drawings follow out systematic consideration of all of the items contained in Part II even at the risk of oversimplification. With experience in the method, greater flexibility and more integrated interpretation will be accomplished particularly as the capacity to coordinate the drawing data with clinical knowledge develops.

Figure 2m and 2f—Schizoid, Obsessive-Compulsive Character

Brief Clinical History: Patient is a twenty-six-year-old white male prisoner convicted of breaking entry into a movie house and stealing a film reel, the showing of which he sat through several times the same day of the offense. The patient had been so fascinated by the bathing beauties in the film that he could not resist the temptation to secure the film for his own private entertainment. This was patient's first brush with the law. Because of the odd nature of the offense and the unusual personality he presented at court, he was referred to the observation wards for study. The patient is a clerical worker and a high school graduate. He tests high average to superior intelligence with a test pattern that is consistent with his schizoid make-up. He is the older of two boys, favored by his mother, and had never married. He was in terror of an authoritarian father who continued to subject him to corporal punishment as if he were still a young child. The patient was sensitive to his poor home environment and to the low cultural standards in the home, but was unable to break away and establish independence in any sphere of adjustment. Instead, he withdrew increasingly into his day-dreams, enriching his fantasy with perfectionist goals. Socially, the patient was quiet, seclusive, and restricted himself to a ruminative interest in music, the fine arts, and in humanity in general. His failure to adjust himself disturbed him, stirring up vague ideas of reference, fearfulness, apprehension, enuresis, and obsessive thoughts. The patient had had no heterosexual contact. Though he was evasive about sexual matters, and generally protective, social contact with the examiner was adequate. Diagnosis was obsessive-compulsive neurosis, schizoid, emotional and psychosexual immaturity.

Drawing Features and Interpretations: Preliminary inquiries of the patient furnished clues to his uncertainty of the sexual role, his reluctance to meet body problems, and

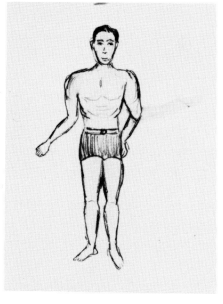

2m

his tendency to evade. Asked to draw a person, he asked: "Man or woman? Profile or full face?"

The succession of parts drawn was irregular, with major attention focussed on physique and body display, and only casual interest and time given to the social and contact features, such as the parts of the face and the hands.

Erasures, line reinforcements, shading, and extreme absorption in the task gave expression to felt anxiety, specific conflicts, and fantasy compensations. Conflict occurred at the shoulders and lower boundary of the ribs (*emphasis on physical power seen in the physically inadequate*). The right hip-line was erased while the left one was reinforced (*confusion at hip-line seen in homosexual conflicts*). The ear sensitivity accords with patient's ideas of reference and his oversensitivity to social opinion. Erasures at the arm

2f

denote conflict as to whether to retreat fully into his own body narcissism or to extend into the social and material environment. Erasures on the female figure were made at the same points as on the male figure, confirming the confusion of male and female body elements existing in the mind of the patient, as well as some degree of identification with both figures in terms of perfection and power.

Erasure of the head with resulting decrease in size of the head is in line with patient's lack of overt aggressiveness in contrast to the fantasy development of social aggression reflected in the rich detailing of the face, coupled with an autistic, "inward" expression. The head is minimized in favor of body power (*treatment common to the obsessive-compulsive whose head, with its control functions, is a most disturbing organ. In this instance, the body impulses won out, culminating in his offense*).

When finished with the male figure, the patient offered it with an embarrassed but self-satisfied smile, remarking, "movie actor." The female figure was identified with the same certainty as, "movie actress." These ego-models express the perfectionism and high fantasy aspirations of the patient. It is of interest that his offense involved movie models.

The drawing of the female figure occupied the better part of an hour with most of the time spent on the shading in an effort to create light effects that would produce the desired transparency. The patient explained that he was trying to produce the effect of an alluring black satin dress. The breasts, stomach, and genital area received most tactile emphasis. The patient smudged, caressed, and modelled with a display of erotic energy that truly made the graphic sexual fantasy very real to him. The facial features and hair received cursory notice in contrast to the attention lavished on the body (*spends most of his recreation time on the beach for the sole purpose of admiring female pulchritude*).

The figure of the man is significantly shorter than that

of the woman. The female figure is given better articulated facial features, more animation and forcefulness, producing the effect of greater social dominance and assertiveness than is attributed the male figure (*emotionally infantile males will frequently make the female image larger and more dominant*).

Although the patient is, in reality, six feet tall, he considers himself short because he had set the perfect height in line with his ego-model, a movie actor. Except for the height of the figure, self-likeness (to the patient) as regards to facial expression and body tensions, is reflected strikingly in the male. The autistic, self-preoccupied expression and the blocked, hesitant, and aborted movement seen in the male figure are characteristic of the patient's bearing.

The reinforced body lines—a knitting together of the body into a tight, compact structure—coincide with patient's feeling of separation from the outside world, and more specifically with his fear of punishment, of castration, and of a threatening sense of body disorganization.

To counteract this fear, we find a very detailed and luxuriant emphasis upon the body, suggesting fantasy regarding body power and self-display. The ego drives are strong, but they have been largely fulfilled in fantasy. All graphic elements of contact with the outside world are weak (*lack of facial animation, extension of appendages is static, hands and feet are encased*).

The finger-and-toe treatment is mildly aggressive in the speared effect, but the rather light line and the encasement indicate the repressed character of the aggression and the blunting of reality contact.

Strong, overdeveloped shoulders are combined with tapering, effeminate arms and legs with tiny wrists and ankles, giving further evidence of the patient's confusion of sexual role with identification blending into perfect female attributes as well as male. The patient's thinking in regard to sex is highly unrealistic.

The special attention given the heel of the foot is similar to the heel emphasis (usually with shoes indicated) on the effeminate male figures done by psychosexually infantile men. It is also in line with the detailed literalism seen in the obsessive character, with corresponding lack of humour and absence of flexibility.

The vague line shading in the chest area signifies the ribs and strength of muscles. The patient himself feels frail, thin, and in imminent danger of some deadly disease. Drive to physical perfection is further emphasized by shoulder reinforcement, selection of a life-guard theme and patient's verbal associations to the male figure.

Emphasis of the margins of the bathing trunks gives evidence of a strong body consciousness with conflict in regard to the concealment and the exhibition of the body. The view that voyeurism is essentially related to the impulse to self-exposure receives some confirmation in this set of drawings. The male figure is exposed, except for a pair of trunks, while the female figure is fully clothed, though with gross transparency. In reality, the patient is over-modest in his attire, while he makes a pastime of viewing partially clothed females on the beach or on the screen.

Emphasis on the buckle, shading at the crotch area, and the rationalized shading of the trunks add to the evidence for sexual consciousness.

The auto-erotic nature of the patient's sexual adaptation is specifically projected in this patient's drawing of the female. The tactile exploitation of the drawing, the patient's effort to achieve his precious transparencies, and his reluctance to terminate the drawing give expression to his sexual fantasies. The vigorous shading of the female figure corresponds with the patient's intense anxiety about his sexual problems, and his relationship to women in general.

The stance of the male is self-conscious, placement on the page is fairly aggressive, and the line is marked by uncertainty, sensitivity, and conflict energy.

One hand behind the back of the female and the other hand towards the body of the female correspond with patient's evasiveness and introversion in regard to his contact with females. He is not frank on that topic.

In associations, the man and woman are both described by the patient as ideal and perfect, with a degree of perfection that relieves him of the obligation to cope with less perfect realities. Associations were given promptly and with enthusiasm, suggesting that the fantasy construction was a real and pleasant experience for the patient. The man is described as being twenty-six (*patient's age*). "He is a life-guard, has perfect physique, is strong-minded, has will power, is a man about town, a man about the beach, has a proud look, and is very glad that he has a manly physique. In other words, he's glad he's what you call a man" (*note the body narcissism, exhibitionism, drive for social dominance, perfectionism, sexual uncertainty and compenstaion for his own obsessive indecision and weakness*). The man is bright and industrious—qualities reflected in the obsessive-compulsive traits characteristic of the patient's drawings (*symmetry, precision, and drive to completion*) and his behavior (*compulsive nature of his offense*). The man works as a blacksmith, using an anvil, and this results in a powerful physique (*note contradictions and poor judgment, when overcome by fantasy drives— the man is a movie actor, a lifeguard, is debonair, and a blacksmith all at the same time*). He is admired by all, is happily married, his wife adores him, and he has two children—a boy and a girl. The woman is described as twenty-one, single, glamorous, dignified. She is a movie star.

3m

Figures 3m and 3f—Paranoid Schizophrenic

Brief Clinical History: This patient is a thirty-nine-year old white male prisoner who is of high average intelligence,

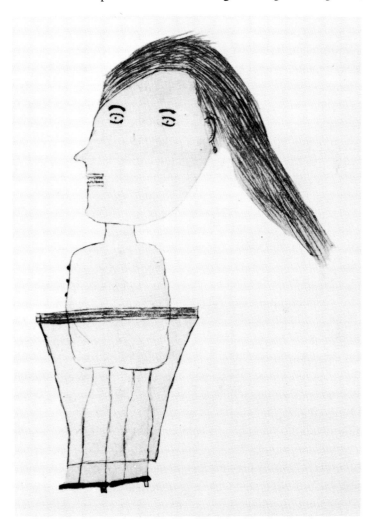

3f

though retarded in school. He was referred for observation because he had come up for re-sentencing on the basis of an old robbery conviction. He had spent many years in an institution for the criminally insane, where he had been transferred from a state prison when he suffered an acute psychotic episode precipitated by a homosexual panic. He was returned to court as improved and capable of standing trial. When seen, the patient was quiet, in good contact, and did not manifest overt psychotic symptoms. The drawings, however, indicated that psychotic processes persisted, though they were quiescent in his present environment. Subsequent probing confirmed the drawing indications, and the patient was diagnosed as a paranoid schizophrenic.

Drawing Features and Interpretation: The schizophrenic flavor of the drawings is seen in the gross disproportion, the emphasis on inessential detail, the static and diagrammatic quality of the figures, the emptiness, confusion of profile, and full face, and the generally bizarre effect of the drawings, all denoting a very private world of ideas.

Patient worked with great interest, absorption, and fantasy preoccupation. He did not follow out a goal, but detailed each area in spatial succession, without any apparent reference to the whole. The break between fantasy and reality, and the absence of insight reflected in the drawings, were further made apparent when patient associated to the figures with sober reflection and consideration of his drawings. He described the male figure as a desirable ego-model of twenty-five, blending his own early background into the verbal image. The female figure was described as a pretty and very desirable girl of seventeen.

The image was related to a niece about whom he had fantasied. He was totally unaware of the true grotesqueness of the figures, even when specifically questioned.

Regression and collapse of judgment are seen in the crude transparency of the lower part of the body in both figures, the confusion of profile and full face, the emphasis on irrelevant details such as buttons and teeth, and the incongruities in the figures.

Paranoid traits are reflected in the rigidity, relatively large size of the drawings, emphasis upon the pin-point eyes, and the aggressive treatment of the fingers. Auditory hallucinations, which patient has experienced in the past, are reflected in the reinforced, transparent, and conspicuous ear treatment.

Symbolic thinking is suggested by the diagrammatic quality of the figures. The patient's ideas of mesmerism, power to influence, and food poisoning were replete with symbolic details. The patient attaches religious symbolic significance to the left and right side of the body. Despite the apparent effort to achieve symmetry, a considerable degree of asymmetry is noted in the treatment of the neck, the head, and the trunk, especially on the male figure. The left and right appendages are treated differently. The right foot was erased many times until a phallic likeness was accomplished. Patient states that he curbs his sexual desires with prayerful meditation. Problems of left and right, sex, and religion are tangled in the patient's mind. The right arm is somewhat longer than the left, does not have the obsessive detailing of finger-nails. It shows more reinforcement (*conflict*) and less restrained aggression than the left (*use of gun and excessive masturbation in history*).

The oral aggression expressed in the diagrammatic mouth and teeth emphasis receives clinical verification in patient's ideas of food poisoning and his stilted and measured speech which, during interview, was reduced to a barely audible pitch.

Emotional dependence, with implications of the authority-submission complex, is seen in the patient's emphasis upon buttons. Buttons feature centrally in his delusions. He relates difficulties encountered with the attendant in the state hospital where he was incarcerated. Whenever the attendant delivered mail to the patient, he presumably noticed that the patient was toying with his buttons. The patient deduced from this that the manipulation of his buttons represented a threat to the attendant to subjugate him sexually, because buttons are prominent on service uniforms and consequently involve subservience. In reality, he was emotionally and psycho-sexually immature and very dependent upon his mother. He never contemplated marriage.

Confusion of sexual role may be noted in the effeminate eyes of the male figure, in the larger size of the female figure, in the confusion of bosom and chest amplitude on the male figure, and in the nail detailing. Sexual conflict is further projected graphically in the shaded trousers which are attached to the body, rather than covering it (*seen in homosexual panic*), the transparency of the female figure below the waistline, the large, erased, and reinforced nose of the male, the phallic-like foot, and the shaded belt speared toward the right (*toward self—patient fears retribution for his homosexual practices*).

Intellectual aspirations suggested by the disproportionately large head, are clinically seen in the patient's pretentious use of the language though he is of limited cultural background. The large head is more pronounced in the female figure. The patient looks upon his mother as a supreme authority. Hair emphasis, generally regarded as a virility indicator, is given the female figure.

Fears of rejection by the mother or by females in general, while having a strong need to be accepted, is the interpretation given the contrast of the long arms on the male figure with the omission of arms on the female. He is greatly concerned about his position as the black sheep in the family.

The uncertainty and apprehension that are clinically manifest are graphically reflected in an uncertain line, uneven pressure, side placement, and the presence of shading.

Body sensitivity to the degree of somatic delusions (*which the patient had had*), is suggested by the emphasis on joints, such as the wrists, elbows, and knees. The midline button theme adds a note of body preoccupation.

Figures 4m and 4f—Normal Child

Brief Clinical History: This is an eight-year old white boy of average intelligence. School progress has been quite poor. It is hampered by a reading disability associated with confusion of lateral dominance (*left handed, right eyed*). This boy has a brother of twelve who is husky and athletic, while he, himself, is frail and girlish. His parents are both working and he is left to shift for himself, or placed in the care of his brother. Standards of feeding and cleanliness are casual, and considerably lower than those of the neighborhood in which he lives. The child is rough with younger children, but withdraws when exposed to competition with his brother. He is shy with adults, is meagre and inhibited in verbal expressiveness, and is infantile in speech.

Drawing Features and Interpretation: Since this child

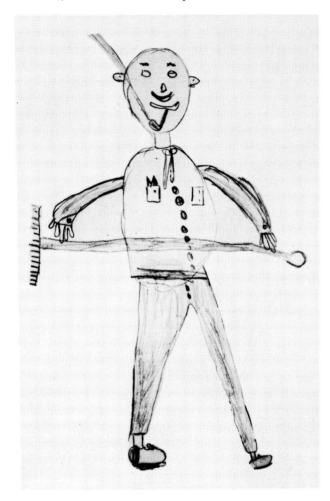

is essentially a motor type, the drawing offered a precious
opportunity for self-expression. He worked with an in-

4f

terest, absorption, detailing, and a sense of reality that he seldom displays in life situations.

Associations to the drawings were a mixture of self-traits, expression of guilt feelings, and wishful thinking. The male figure is described as ten, strong, and good-looking, but has crooked arms (*subject is left-handed and shows confusion of dominance*). The figure is an actor and is reading poems (*the child is retiring and backward in school and is not called upon for recitations*). The boy likes his mother best because she does not spank him (*identification with the mother is marked in child's behavior*). The head is described as the best part of the body (*scholastic retardates place much emphasis upon the functions of the head. In addition, this subject is "pretty" and may stress the head on the basis that girls do*). The boy would like to get married when he grows up, but he is too small and too dirty to ever get married (*subject is dirty and small*). The worst part of the boy is that he doesn't flush the toilet (*true of subject*). He has a sister of fourteen (*subject would prefer an older sister as "assistant mother" to supervision by his brother*). Associations to the girl figure describe her as the older sister of the boy figure. She is fourteen. She makes "tumblesauces," doesn't eat her lunch, and will grow up to be an artist (*all true of subject*). The subject concludes his associations to the girl with "artist, that's me" (*this distribution of self-traits between the male and female figures has been noted in individuals who show confusion in regard to their sexual role, though it is fairly normal for young children*).

Active fantasy is seen in the large size of the figures, the wealth of detail, the diligence of application, reluctance to leave the task until he was fully satisfied, and the degree of symbolic content that is involved. Space is used courageously with a spreading out of the figures and arms, reaching out towards the environment (*urge to participate socially blocked by child's timidity*).

The lines used are uneven in pressure and solidity, suggesting tension, uncertainty, and emotional instability.

Facial features (*impulse for social contact*) are well articulated (*subject is always looking for someone to play with or for adult attention*).

The full face view is consistent with the subject's age, mental level, and accessibility concerning his problems.

The figures tip towards the right with the unevenness of legs, arms, shoulders, and general disturbance in symmetry that has been noted in confusion of lateral dominance cases.

Large feet and long legs are more characteristic of boys' than of girls' drawings. The personal record of this subject supports the interpretation that insecurity and a drive for competitive action and physical growth may account for the sex difference.

Special emphasis on features relating to virility striving is to be seen in the mustache, the pipe (*though the figure is only supposed to be ten years old*), a small tie, shaded belt emphasis, and a large, anxiously shaded rake which has no functional significance congruent with the figure (*phallic significance?*). Feelings of sexual inadequacy (*perhaps in comparison with his brother*) and preoccupation in that sphere (*masturbation*) are suggested by the tiny fragment of a tie and the buttons on the fly of the trousers (*subject feels inferior in all respects and is regarded as a sissy*).

The force of the fantasy throws the figure into illogical development. The figure is dressed up with a tie and conspicuous handkerchief although he is presumably planting (*subject is sensitive about his raggedness*). Contradictions in childrens' drawings are, however, common, since children often tend to project their problems in different areas, regardless of coherence or consistency. In this particular instance, lack of consistency and illogic are individually characteristic of the subject.

Button emphasis along the midline of the trunk corresponds with subject's body sensitivity and his extreme dependence upon his mother.

The shading of the legs is regarded as anxiety about size and physical growth.

The shading of the arms is related to the unsatisfactory and anxious nature of subject's contacts with scholastic materials and to a general feeling of failure in his contacts with his social environment.

The prominence of the ear may be coordinated with subject's sensitivity to criticism and to his hunger for social approval (*he is often observed off in a corner, listening intently*).

Pocket emphasis in both male and female figures is coordinated with the subject's mother dependence, affectional, and in the subject's mind, perhaps material deprivation (*subject is ill-kempt and neglected*).

The highly original treatment of the pockets on the female figure suggests a libidinal concentration on the mother. The face of "Joe" (*the subject*) and "Fox" (*the brother's name is Fred*) are drawn in the pockets and placed in the position of the breasts. The full figures of the two are drawn underneath. "Joe" is made twice as large as "Fox," although in reality, Joe, the subject, is the younger of the two boys.

The figure of the girl is smaller than that of the boy, although she is described as four years older than the boy (*the need for the subject to become as big as his brother. The difference between the subject and his older brother is also four years*). The girl drawn is presumably wearing a Halloween party dress. Note the position of the decorations on the girl and where the box is held. The girls that decorate the dress are described by subject as going to school with their schoolbox (*school is a source of frustration to this subject. He feels that better marks will make him more acceptable to his mother*).

Food emphasis is seen in the drawing of the table with lunch set on it (*the mother always leaves lunch on the table for him*). In the associations, the worst thing about the girl is that she doesn't eat (*true of subject*). The extremely wide mouth on both figures gives further graphic testimony to subject's oral problems. The dog underneath the table is given a coat to protect him (*subject identifies himself as the underdog in the family. There are also several dogs in the house, despite the neglect of the children*).

The male figure is given no hair except for a mustache (*father is bald*) while the female is given all sorts and directions of haircomb (*mother is the dominant member in the household. She is younger and more virility is assigned to her*).

The female is given more aggressive fingers than the male.

The eyes of both figures show large orbits, but have no pupils, or seeing mechanism (*subject is undiscriminating,*

*has little factual knowledge, and no precision—the environ-
ment is experienced "en masse"*).

The shape of the decoration at the genital area of the
female which was erased and reinforced (*conflict*), is
suggestive of the star of David (*subject's father is Jewish.
His mother is a Gentile*).

The line enclosing the chest area of both figures is
more disturbed than other lines in the drawing (*related to
subject's sense of physical frailty?*).

Figures 5m and 5f—Acute Adolescent Crisis

Brief Clinical History: This patient is a sixteen-year old
white prisoner of average intelligence and normal school
progress. He was referred to the hospital because of his
persistent running away and car stealing. The patient was
adopted by two maiden social workers when he was
twelve. Recently, he has become moody, irascible, and
unmanageable. He was extremely resentful of his guardians' efforts to treat him as mentally ill. His only wish
was to be reunited with his mother from whom he had
been kept for eight years. He declares that this wish is
his motive for his runaways. The home background of
the patient is friction-ridden. It is a patchwork of step-
fathers, stepmothers, and foster-mothers; he is confused
about his loyalties. He is further confused by the different
names given to him by the various guardians. The present
picture is that of a harassed, apprehensive adolescent who
is functioning poorly and is burdened with guilt feelings.
There is a vacillating identification with an errant father
whom he hopes to replace in his mother's life. Diagnosis
was that of adolescent crisis in a neurotic boy with emotional and psychosexual immaturity.

Drawing Features and Interpretation: Drawings were done reticently with preliminary questioning — "whole body or only the face?" Patient made a line drawing at first for the male, giving only the midline axis and legs (*reluctance to meet the problems that are agitating him*).

5m

Pants were then added and the body was given dimensions. The arms followed diffidently (*contact with environment*), and finally the head was drawn (*fear of meeting the interpersonal problem*). The female figure was also drawn in irregular succession (*disturbed logic*), beginning with the tiny feet and working up timidly and cautiously toward the head (*the future of patient's relationship toward his real mother was a moot point*).

The theme of the drawing is a rather dramatic projection of the patient's current behavior. The male figure is described by the patient as running for a bus to go to work (*patient has indeed felt torn between conflicting allegiances*

*and projected demands and has been running away from
it all. On card V of the Rorschach, he saw "two animals
at the side, rushing at the rabbit in the middle." He has
been further anxious to establish himself at work to support his mother).* The male figure was described as good-

5f

looking and well dressed (*patient's aspiration*), but not too
strong (*true of patient. He is thin and frail*). He is a
lawyer, twenty-nine years old, and unmarried (*aspiration
to replace father*). He satisfies himself sexually by mas-
turbating (*conflict of patient. In discussing sex, he referred
to the mysterious relationship between the two maiden
women who adopted him*).

Insecurity, inadequacy, and fear are reflected in the light, broken, and uneven line. These characteristics are also seen in the bewildered facial expression, in the small and slight figure (*same as patient*), in the fearful approach to the body image, in the faint feet on the male figure and the tiny feet on the female figure.

Midline emphasis, marked by the original heavy line done for the body, corresponds with the body inferiority and self-preoccupation that are clinically apparent.

Reaching out for the love of his mother is suggested by the long, outstretched arms, while uncertainty of acceptance by her is seen in the short arms of the female figure.

The omission of hands would relate to patient's guilt regarding his car stealing and also regarding his lack of achievement (*guilt aggravated by the demands of his guardians*). He had never made an adequate adjustment to people or things.

Poor standards of achievement, restlessness, and poor judgment are denoted by the transparencies and incompletions in the male figure.

Beginning the drawing with an approximation of an armature suggests a drive for perfectionism that is associated with obsessive-compulsive traits (*patient's search for his mother and persistent car-stealing were quite compulsive in character*). The midline and symmetry theme, often associated with these traits, is more pronounced in the front view given the female figure.

The greatest amount of transparency occurs beneath the waistline of the male figure—an area in which his judgment may be extremely poor (*the man is described as having established a satisfactory sex life on an auto-*

erotic level). An interesting accent of interest in sexuality is indicated by the brief and irrelevant lines in the skirt of the female.

The heavy line encasing the chest and the restless shading assigned to that region are consistent with patient's sense of physical inferiority and weakness.

Mother fixation and confusion of sexual role find expression in the markedly larger female figure, the greater detailing given her, the longer neck, and the reinforced shoulders (*physical power*). The dominance of the female figure is especially significant in view of patient's description of that figure as a girl eleven years younger than the male. She is described as perfect, brilliant, beautiful, and an unattainable sex object. Libidinization of the mother image is corroborated in clinical study of the patient with corresponding emotional and psychosexual retardation. The clothing is suitable to a mother type.

The patient's guardians had suspected that he was a developing schizophrenic, but the drawing analysis leans more towards the diagnosis that was finally made—acute adolescent crisis in a neurotic boy whose physical and environmental background has contributed to unwholesome development. His strong inner drive for social assertion (*reinforced profile*) and his aspiration (*reinforced forehead, man is described as a lawyer, and pressure by guardians for achievement*) has found only fantasy expression, resulting in cumulating frustration.

Figures 6m and 6f—Schizophrenic Excitement, Manic Features

Brief Clinical History: This is a thirty-eight year old white male who was admitted to the hospital in an excite-

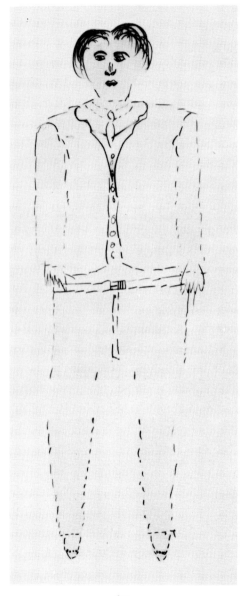

6m

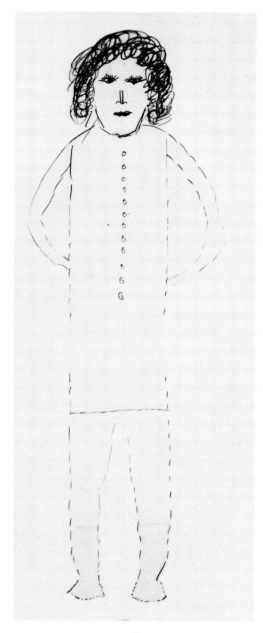

6f

ment characterized by both manic and schizophrenic features. Acute onset of his illness was coincidental with a crisis that had developed in his work relations several months prior to admission. His work as a lens grinder left him in poor health at the same time that he suffered a change in personality in the direction of inactivity and even mutism. This was soon followed by overtalkativeness, loss of a life-long stutter, regression to archaic number symbolisms, ideas of grandeur, religious powers and paranoid ideas involving intrigue and spies. When he was examined, he appeared more serious, self-absorbed, and more insulated than the usual manic. Throughout his tendency to scatter in his productions, he managed to maintain a logical thread. He combined agitation, bewilderment, and apprehension with his grandiosity. He was essentially friendly, though irritable when crossed. He had received several electric shock treatments in a private sanitarium, but these were discontinued because he was so generally unmanageable. He died of exhaustion shortly after his transfer to a state hospital. He had been married, had one child, was of superior intelligence, and a high school graduate. Prior to his marriage, he lived with his mother and sister. The father had deserted the home. He associated his numerical compulsion to count by three plus one with the family unit of three, plus the absent father. He stated that he is now doing penance for the sin committed against his mother by marrying.

Drawing Features and Interpretation: Drawing was accepted by him after some hesitation (*reluctance to be confronted with his problems*). He then asked to have a ruler with which to draw a midline accurately (*midline emphasis checks with patient's egocentricity and somatic preoccupations. The need to maintain accuracy, or perfectionist drive with the use of a ruler gives testimony to a decompensating obsessional system that can no longer be trusted to exercise control).* The paper was then folded into the three magical parts that characterized the patient's number obsession (*a further prop to control the unknown. It is also barely possible that the three horizontal parts refer symbolically to the various levels of the personality*). These ritualistic preliminaries completed, patient inquired whether he should draw a man or a woman, and without waiting for an answer, proceeded to draw a woman first. When he completed the head of the woman, he remarked that she looked more like a man (*reinforcing the impression of conflict as regards to patient's sexual role*). Though patient's attention wandered, and he frequently digressed, he completed the drawing on his own volition (*suggesting that the psychic datum upon which he drew for his image was fixed and well established, and did not depend upon immediate concentration*). When he reached the bottom of the page in his drawing of the female, he asked if he should complete it. A second page was put within his reach without comment. Patient continued his drawing on this page (*inner compulsion to complete a task in which he was not interested and in which no examiner-pressure was exerted*).

Succession of both male and female figures was very irregular, proceeding in a manner that satisfied the patient's internal logic. On the female figure, drawing began with abundant and chaotic treatment of the hair (*sexual vitality and freedom*). In his associations, the patient said: "Woman doesn't need man—just for a plaything—she could have a child even today without intercourse. She is favored by God." The hair was followed by aggressive, hostile, and menacing facial features (*the social dominance and power given to the female by infantile males*). A strong, reinforced chin followed (*decisiveness and determination*). The patient proceeded in a stimulus-bound, chain-association fashion, developing each spatial area in small sections, bilaterally. (*He is too confused about interpersonal relationships to permit a spontaneous approach to the goal idea of a "person." This piecemeal, bilateral treatment is similar to the props and rituals used as a substitute for control by obsessive characters.*) When the patient reached the bottom of the dress, he commented: "I don't know how long to make it." He then erased the bottom line, and lengthened the figure (*in line with the exaggerated image of graphic size and power invested in the female and substantiated in patient's associations*). When he approached the feet, he protested: "I don't know how!" He then added the feet with a change of line (*conflict area*).

The feet of the female are more like animal hoofs, in contrast to the effeminate and refined feet given the male figure (*the foot as a penis symbol receives considerable support in this set. The female, in contrast to the male, is given the animal power and freedom of sexuality, corresponding with the hair treatment*).

The patient's fragmented line may be regarded in terms of discrete counting, as a ritual and obsessive necessity. The broken line further permits a fluidity of environmental exchange with an unintegrated and insecure body image. It would allow for the escape and evaporation of body impulses, while not offering protection against the hazards of the environment. Although the outlines in regard to individual body parts are clearly delineated, there is no solid wall of demarcation of the figure as a whole. The patient finally did succumb fatally to exhaustion from the struggle against progressive disintegration. Castration fears were expressed by him directly: "The man had lost his penis use. It had shrunk to seven inches because of misuse in white slavery, filth, disease, and intercourse during menstrual periods."

The size of both drawings is excessively large (*corresponding with the grandiosity, fantasy, manic trends, and paranoid features in the clinical picture*).

The placement on the page is in the middle with fairly wide and assertive stance (*aggression and the obsessive drive to centralization and symmetry corresponding with features repeatedly substantiated in drawing and clinical traits*).

The female with her hands on the hips, her vertical, masculine body, her size, chaotic disarray of hair, and menacing facial expression represents a formidable and castrating mother-image. The patient described her as forty—"she lives forever in my vision," while the male figure is twenty-four (*a mother-son relationship in respect to graphic features and patient's associations*).

Asked to draw a man, the patient remarked: "A man must be smaller." The male figure was described by him as the son of the female he drew. The nicest part of his body is his face (*patient is goodlooking*). Questioned about the worst part, he asked: "About sex or what?" (*preoccupation with castration*). He has nice shoulders (*compensation for feelings of physical inferiority*). Though the patient was impressed by the man's big shoulders, he regarded him as very intelligent as well (*perfect in all but sexual spheres*). He regarded the arm as too short, since, he argued, it should be the length of the leg (*the arm as a penis symbol?*) When the patient was asked if the male was married, he sighed and began to chant, "three times four, three times four, three times four," and finally decided the man had a wife and son (*same as patient*). He resorted to this numerical ritual when answering questions relating to marriage, sex, or to his mother. He measured the fly on the trousers to indicate that in the resurrection, which the patient has the power to perform, the man's penis will be thirteen inches, twelve plus one. The first detail that he drew on the male body was the buckle, with three vertical lines and one horizontal line (*the three plus one theme*). He followed with lines on the fly of the trousers, counting them altogether as thirteen.

After leaving the sexual area, he drew a meagre tie with heavy pressure (*aggressive reaction to weak sexuality*).

He changed, confused, and erased lines around the neck (*conflict in regard to the control of raw impulses*).

The belt was then drawn with heavy pressure and the outlines of the jacket received positive and reinforced treatment (*body consciousness with repressed exhibitionistic trends—must keep body securely wrapped up*).

The buttons were then added (*marked mother dependence*), with counting of "three times four" on the female figure and "twice three plus one" on the male figure (*number rituals in context of discussion of sex or mother relationships*).

Erasures occurred only to lengthen the height of the female, and to widen the lapel-opening on the male to give display to the small tie (*the patient is too full of a sense of reality in his fantasy projection to erase very much).*

The fingers on the male figure are speared (*aggression*) and, on the female, the hand is evaded (*an element of cutting off the female power to punish?*).

The arms of the male figure are pressed close to the body (*withdrawal, tension, and holding body together*), while those of the female are placed in a rejective and punitive position, but are given initial direction away from the body (*extraverted aspects of the female image?*).

The lips of the male figure are more effeminate than those of the female.

The nose of the male is shaded (*castration fear*) and shuts out the smells of the world in its convex curve of the nostrils, while, on the female, the nose is sharp and aquiline and has a concave, or receptive curve to the nostrils.

The expression of the face and the figure of the female are menacing, while, though some aggressive indications are contained in the male figure, the expression is primarily one of weakness and bewilderment (*the exact expression of this patient clinically*).

The neck is emphasized in the male, but the female is given no neck (*less inhibited and conflicted in regard to the expression of her impulses*). The patient stated that during the six thousand years of civilization, man had lost the use of his penis. The identification of his wife with his mother is given in this statement: "When man will be resurrected, he will be given two women, one older, one younger. One would cook for him and play with him in the morning, and one would be for the afternoon."

Emphasis upon symmetry and midline is marked in the male figure) (*obsessional and somatic stress*). The male's hair treatment is more meagre and orderly than that of the female (*more inadequate and more restrained virility*).

The patient spontaneously recorded the male figure as twenty-four years (*both paranoid and manic patients do spontaneous writing and identification*).

Figures 7m and 7f—Normal Female

Brief Clinical History: The subject was thirty-four years of age and single at the time the drawings were made. She had, for ten years, maintained a close friendship with a man who was older and weaker in personality than herself. She is the only girl and the youngest of three children. Though of good native ability, she was indifferent to school, allowing her brothers to excel her in educational attainment. Intellectual aspirations of the family were focussed upon a favored brother. In her particular family unit being the only girl gave no privileges, but only tended to foster a sense of uselessness. Her mother was an uneducated, infantile personality given to intense narcissism, grandiose and nostalgic daydreaming, fantasy aspirations for wealth and distinction, and occasional outbursts of hysterical aggression. The subject resembled her mother physically, in her pretenses and aspirations, and her egocentricity. Her father, on the other hand, was mild, introverted, given to bookreading and few outside interests. The family unit lacked harmony or warmth. What warmth she had was focussed upon the father. She was embarrassed by the modest cultural and economic standards of the home, and lived her social life outside of it. Upon the death of the mother, several years prior, she moved promptly into the mother's position in the household, although a housekeeper was maintained. She continued to receive support from her elderly father, although she was in excellent health and the employment market was maximal. Her employment prior to this, was never more than a gesture, since she was never able to maintain her extravagant clothes and superficial display of wealth with her meagre earnings. The mother had always groomed her for a wealthy marriage. She was superficially sociable, but not friendly. Details of her sexual history are unknown.

7m

Drawing Features and Interpretation: This subject accepted drawings with some self-consciousness (*she is evasive and not easily given to confidences*). She interpreted the direction to "draw a person" as "draw a man"

7f

(*point of sexual ambivalence and confusion of identifica-tion*). Before starting, she asked: "Must I draw hands?" (*The subject was vocationally not self-maintaining and was uncertain about social and sexual contacts*). After these preliminaries (*hesitant in adjusting to a situation*), she became engrossed in the task (*much fantasy and inner living to project, evidenced by her addiction to movies and romantic novels, and borne out in her ready associations to the drawings*).

She drew the head outline, remarking: "I could only draw a face. I certainly can't draw feet!" (*Her social facade and personal appearance have constituted her ego front. Sexual and vocational adaptations, which are func-tionally involved in other parts of the body, have been weak. Insecurity of footing is both graphically and clinic-ally outstanding*).

As she was finishing the facial features, she remarked: "He has a young face and is prematurely bald," though both figures are described as adolescent in her associations (*both her boyfriend and father are partially bald*). The head is finally given hair and the drawing develops into a female (*sexual ambivalence*). Shoulder pads are given much emphasis by extension and erasures (*broad shoulders of a male—confusion of sexual attributes and of sexual identification*). From that point on, the succession of both drawings shows no gross irregularities (*capable of logical thinking with conventional overtones in neutral areas*).

The direction of the arms presented a problem which was expressed in much erasing and alteration without im-provement of form. Her final solution was to put them behind the back (*always uncertain about the degree of participation in the environment—conflicted by pull to narcissistic fantasy and self-indulgence-compromise results in evasion and concealment which is characteristic of her).*

The hair style on the female is reminiscent of a picture of this subject which was taken when she was approximately the age assigned to the figure. The hair style is tight and compact (*effort at restraint*), but essentially fuzzy and very dark in line pressure (*impulse to primitive and free sexuality turned into anxious aggression*). The hair covers most of the forehead (*suggests dependence upon sexual vitality and allure for social appeal rather than upon intellectual attainment*). It is of interest to recall that a similar hair style which covered the forehead was prevalent during the flapper days after World War I. This was coincidental with the definite trends toward the underplaying of intellect and the stressing of "low-brow" sexual abandon. She had probably been discouraged in achieving dominance through scholarship by the presence of accomplished brothers in the home, and had gravitated toward non-intellectual ways of achieving mastery early in her development.

The subject states in her associations that the worst thing that she did was to hit her little brother, of whom she is very jealous because he is getting all the attention. Although financially subsidized by her family, the subject was not favored by them. Sibling rivalry may have contributed to the confusion of the sexual role apparent in the drawings. In reality, she has taken on all the accoutrements of femininity to the point of overpreening. The drawings suggest that she tends to use this femininity to fulfill the masculine drive for domination and free self-expression. In the drawings, the girl is austere, prim, unadorned, large in size (*high self-esteem*), is placed assertively on the page and shows a fairly aggressive stance. The exhibitionism and narcissism that characterize her behavior are, in the drawings, converted into aggression, determination, challenge, and some degree of sadness. One may conjecture therefrom that she resents having to achieve mastery indirectly, through feminine wiles.

The dim line, uncertain footing, and dependence suggested by the emphatic buckle, and the hiding of the hands (*guilt and lack of confidence*), are graphic elements that belie the self-assertive stance.

The long arms (*ambition*) and the wide shoulders (*physical power drive*) are counteracted by anxious lines for the legs. The subject regards the legs as the worst part of the female (*though she has nice legs herself, she is inactive athletically, is not mobile in her day's routine, and probably feels she is going nowhere*). The feet were special sources of disturbance (*insecurity, no mooring*). After preliminary resistance to them, she omitted them with a show of active annoyance. She recovered however, with an aggressive scribble which she rationalized as "tall grass" (*the subject did indeed let tall grass grow around her feet in every sphere of adaptation, and is aggressively defensive on that point*).

The bitter expression of the female may reflect her true reaction to an unrequited fantasy of romantic and glamourous attainments—a fantasy in which she was nurtured since early childhood by her mother. Only a shadow of this fantasy was left in her barren life. The sadness and sterility of the figure are offset by the theme of birds (*flight fantasy*), a tree (*reproduction—an aggressive and barren male symbol as the patient drew it*), and "the girl is walking" (*movement impulse seen in individuals who rely on fantasy, especially since movement is counteracted in the female figure by hands behind the back and rigidity of the figure).*

The figure was described as an awkward girl of seventeen (*the emotional and psychosexual maturity of this subject did not develop beyond the adolescent level*). The girl is full of dreams about her boyfriend. She is serious and preoccupied (*The subject's fear of adulthood—hesitant acceptance of female sexuality*). She is close to her mother, but is crazy about her father (*true of subject*). She is wealthy and is at her country home (*wealth and leisure important to the subject*), and she is as popular as she wants to be (*the subject is defensive about interpersonal relationships*). The girl is further identified with the heroine of a book bearing the morbid title, "Dynasty of Death" (*identification with fiction characters. Dysphoric title is in line with the sadness of the female figure and the actual life of the subject*).

Much emphasis is given the facial features (*social aspect*), but they are, in effect, serious, set, and introverted (*fantasy nature of much of her impulse for social communicability and domination*). The introduction of a theme, the size and aggression of the figure, and the intention toward movement, suggest a degree of fantasy enterprise which offers contrast to the low level of activity and enterprise in the behavior of the subject. Elements which further support the impression of conflict between this gravitation toward fantasy and the necessity to meet facts are seen in her niggardly and barren treatment in elaboration of this fantasy. The birds, the tall grass, the tree, the necklace, hair ribbon, the breasts, and figure curves (*though the girl's ambition is described by her as "to become a wife and mother"*), are all given meagre and restrained graphic attention in contrast to the profuse verbal fantasy.

The necklace is a tight choker that serves more as a line of separation between the body (*impulses*) and the head (*control functions*), than to adorn the figure. The neck is also relatively long.

In her associations, the subject was uncertain as to whether the background of the female was autumn or spring (*she is worried about that in her own life. Drawn to the spring of a schoolgirl of seventeen, she is, in reality, feeling autumn approaching*).

The head features are consistently darker than body outlines (*stress upon fantasy and social front while avoiding body conflicts*).

Darker lines are also used in other conflict areas. The phallic-like symbol of the broken, speared, and jagged tree, the buckle (*mother-dependence, sexual pre-occupation*), and the grass (*rationalization of insecure footing*) are done with considerable pressure of line.

The male figure, in which the subject projects aspects of herself (*spread of traits between male and female figures seen in the sexually uncertain*) is an actual likeness of a cousin who had been raised in her home as a younger brother (*the subject was not conscious of the resemblance in the drawing and in the associations*). The figure is described as seventeen, a senior at Brooklyn Technical High School (*note the "BTHS" is reinforced and exhibitionistically displayed—facts check with the boy that the drawing resembles*). He is an only child, closer to the father (*wish of subject*). He is further described as on the cheering squad and girls are crazy about him (*popu-*

larity craved by subject). His father is an athlete from Princeton (*aspiration for family culture*), and plans to take the boy into business (*assured and subsidized future given to the male, in contrast to the female, dreaming of such future*).

The subject stresses physique in her description of the male figure, while, in the drawing, though assigned the same age, the male is made substantially smaller than the female and less powerful. Further confusions indicating conflict between fantasy and fact are seen in the large head given the male (*leaves intellectuality to the male*) while, in the verbal description of him, he is given more physique and popularity, than sensitivity or brains. He is also given a relatively short neck (*better coordination of physical and mental life than the female*). He is more handsome, more popular, has a more assured future, and has to rely less on daydreams than the female. Although the male is described as an extravert by the subject, his facial (*social*) features are less pronounced than those of the female. He is intended as a "rah! rah!" boy: "I'll make him excited—surprised." But the drawing reflects reserve and inner rebellion similar to the female figure. The male figure is given a pronounced Adam's apple which appears as a reinforced tie-knot. He is further given a BTHS athletic symbol and reinforced shoulders to sustain the virility that the subject assigns to him in her verbal picture of him, but which the graphic image lacks so sadly. A psychic interruption in the flow of line around the hips of both figures suggests confusion of male and female characteristics. Change of line and erasures of the crotch area of the male mark the area of sexual conflict.

The male is given shorter arms than the female (*less*

enterprise and ambition). He is given more security of role in the verbal associations.

Emphasis of margins of clothing in the male refers somewhat to the subject's own conflict between modesty and impulse to display. In behavior, this may be reflected in overrestraint, combined with drives to ostentatious pretenses.

The feet are drawn dimly and small in size with detailed shoe treatment (*in contrast to no feet in the female*), with special attention given to the heel (*shoe and foot treatment effeminate in all respects*) and double outline of the length of the shoe (*penis symbolization?*).

Unusual care is also given the ear of the male (*refers to oversensitivity of the subject, especially in regard to the opposite sex*). The patient gave verbal emphasis to the ear with the remark: "That's why I made a woman out of the man in the first place. I didn't know what do do with the ear" (*she always likes to appear insensitive to opinion, self-assured, and lacking in conflict*).

In actual fact, the subject's relationship to the cousin whom the male figure resembles has been both as mother-child attachment, and as competition for the affection of the father with a much younger brother (*in associations, the girl was jealous of a much younger brother*). The male is attributed less conflict than the female in her associations, while the graphic images run in the opposite direction. Both figures and the verbal descriptions given them, project the wishful thinking, sentiments, and frustrations of the subject as well as her conflict in acceptance of the feminine role.

Figures 8m and 8f—Normal Male

Brief Clinical History: The subject is a twenty-six year old male, single, has attended evening college for two years, and has held only unskilled and sporadic jobs prior to army service. He was never in combat areas, though he was abroad for several years. Since his return, he has been idle and totally lacking in ambition or goal. He displays no overt anxiety about his listlessness, but since he has not been explored clinically, his inner feelings are not known. He responds with superficial congeniality when exposed to social relationships, but he does not seek them out. His only spontaneous interest is baseball. His social life is restricted to visits to the family with his mother. He appears physically and emotionally immature, although he is above average in intelligence and has a moderately good physique. He is growing stout from inactivity and over-eating. His food interests are restricted along the line of the infantile pattern of what was served to him by his mother. He is indifferent about the evening college courses which he attends, accepting them as a sort of refuge that he is satisfying family standards of education. Recent contact with this subject found him retreating increasingly into his body functions with emphasis upon special food, and upon every minute sensation. Verbalized goals are vague, shifting, and lacking in conviction. He is the youngest of three boys. The brother next in line is considered independent, witty, bright, and socially compelling. He was always openly favored. The oldest boy is solid and reliable, though shy and passive. He had made an exemplary adjustment in the army, and had recently married. The subject grew in this shadow of better adjusted and more openly accepted brothers. He had given up the competitive challenge early in his development, when an injury to his shoulder cut short his ambition to become a professional baseball player. Though he is close to his mother, he seems to be accepted as a dependent and

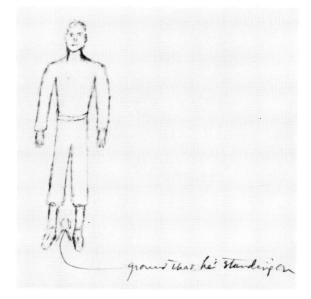

ground that he standing on

8m

obedient child rather than a loved or respected one. He was deeply homesick in the army. When he was of pre-school age, he handled his sibling rivalry with destructive aggressiveness, earning frequent criticism, punishment and rejection by all in his environment. Sexually, he has never been known to have a date with a girl.

Drawing Features and Interpretation: The subject accepted the task with the question: "Whole or part?" (*fear of facing the body problems which he has managed to evade by inactivity*). He was hesitant and apologetic about his drawing (*although his skill is relatively good—chronic lack of confidence*). He drew the head cautiously (*some apprehension, fear of commitment, and restrained aggression in social contacts*). He filled in the facial features

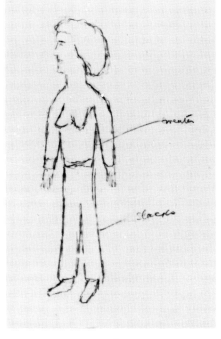

8f

dimly (*unassertive and shy in surface contact*). A faint indication of hair on the head was rapidly erased but was given no more abundance when altered (*virility is definitely uncertain and weak with conflict expressed in erasures*). The eyes are small (*afraid to see?*) and are darker (*aggressive emphasis*) than the other features (*furtive sexual curiosity and voyeuristic interests have been suspected in him*). The ears were given substantial emphasis with reinforcement of the left ear (*he is sensitive to criticism and to opinion of others*). The subject then proceeded to the neck and shoulders, which he promptly erased and reinforced (*conflict areas*), giving an extra line to the chin (*the neck refers to difficulty in coordinating impulse life with the control and inhibitive functions of the head. The shoulders show concentration on body development, and the chin is compensation for indecisiveness*). He completed the trunk and added arms and hands before continuing with the lower half of the body (*perhaps avoidance of sexual area*). He worked in a bilateral fashion with small units drawn symmetrically from side to side (*seen in obsessionals—fear of leaving the spatial-bound security to enterprise a large area or goal idea all at one time*). He remarked that the hands, "look like claws." The hands and fingers are dimmed, but reinforcements are noticeable with the general effect of being tense, weighed down, and laden (*fear of aggressive impulses in addition to guilt regarding masturbation which is confirmed by associations to the figure*). There is no flexibility in the hand (*weak vocational adaptation*). If one looks closely, a heavy accent of aggression may be noted as drawn deliberately on some of the left finger-tips. After completing the legs and feet, he added some ground (*prop for security of footing*) and inquired—"Is that enough?"—with a sense of relief.

Erasures and special line pressure are to be seen at the crotch (*sexual preoccupation of an auto-erotic nature in this subject*).

The midline emphasis on the feet gives an additional obsessional note to that expressed by the almost rigid symmetry of the figure and the bilateral succession in drawing (*midline and special detail treatment of the shoe of the male figure is frequent in drawings of adolescent girls).*

The midline (*somatic preoccupation*) in the male figure is treated cautiously (*the subject does not accept his mother-dependence and somatic withdrawal without conflict*) with a few indications of buttons (*mother dependence*) and an Adam's apple (*masculinity striving*).

The wide dimension of the contour lines of the body suggests an insulation from the environment and retreat into the body (*true of subject*), but the lightness and porousness of the line combined with erasures and reinforcements (*marking conflict areas*) and the tension of the figure, give a vulnerable and sensitive tone to the figure, indicating felt conflict.

The rather thin body may relate to his preoccupation about his adding weight due to his inactivity (*compensatory treatment*).

A subtle psychic interruption in the form of reinforcement of line is noted on the right side of the hip-line (*an area commonly emphasized by sexually confused adults*).

Placement of the figure is a bit off to the left (*introversive*) side, but the stance is fairly assertive for all the line tensions and need for grounding (*he does make adequate social contact when he is engaged*).

The proportions of the figure are quite normal, except for a slight favoring of body power through broadening of the shoulders.

The impression of clothing is that of a baseball uniform, but that was not checked with the subject. (*He was trying for professional baseball at the age given the figure.*)

Associations describe him as seventeen; he has only a younger sister (*resentment against older brothers*), is above average intelligence, is strong, and the best part of him is his face and build; the worst part is his stiffness. He likes athletics, doesn't know what he will be in the future, prefers to be with boys, has never had sex with girls or boys, and is disgusted with his masturbatory habit (*all true of subject*). The legs are his worst feature; they have no muscles (*subject has strong legs, but this may refer to his sense of insecurity and inactivity*). The verbal picture fixes the age of the male figure at the threshold of adulthood—the point at which the subject has been emotionally fixated.

The female figure, on the other hand, has, in associations to it given by this subject, been allowed to go on to maturity. He describes her as twenty-six or twenty-seven (*his own age*). She is looking off into the distance (*a habit of his*). She is married and has a son of five (*some vacillation on that point*). She is a housewife, had some college, is goodlooking, and has a slender figure (*wish of subject for himself*). Her best feature is her friendliness (*true of subject*); her worst part is her flat feet (*subject complains of flat feet*). After giving her slacks and, except for prominent breasts, a rather masculine figure, he remarks that she is "too feminine; not enough of a tomboy" (*confusion of sexual traits related to infantile nurturance dependence*). Her husband is in the army, she reminds him of several women in the neighborhood, and he would like a woman like that for himself (*subject has undoubtedly had fantasies in regard to some of the women in the neighborhood whose husbands were overseas*).

Preliminary remarks and comments, while drawing the female, were significant. He asked if the profile was all right (*evasiveness in meeting the female problem*). He sketched the profile with the same gingerly tension that he did the male features of the face (*extreme shyness in presence of females*). He then remarks: "This is going to be a picture of a tomboy" (*more reluctance to meet the girl problem*). He drew the hair and neck and erased and reinforced at the same points as in the male figure (*again problems of sexual virility and coordination of mental and physical activities enter*). He followed with the shoulders, arms and hands, erasing the shoulders (*physical power-confusion of sexual characteristics*), and treating the hands with the same finger-tip accent that he did the male (*stasis of activity may be partially due to obsessional fears of resuming the aggressive and destructive pattern of contact that he formed in his early childhood. Also, the considerable spread of self-traits between the male and female figure is here emphasized, indicating confusion of sexual role*). He reached the breast area of the female with: "Now I'm really stuck. Am I supposed to dress this woman too?" (*sexual curiosity and perhaps voyeuristic trends expressed in his interest in pornography*). The final result of this conflict was a compromise with what appears as unclothed breasts. He erased, changed the line, and, before the drawing was given up, returned to the breasts for additional reinforcement of line (*the conflict centering around that area is obvious. It gives the background of mother fixation, oral deprivation and rejection, as the source of his psychosexual retardation*). When he finished the trunk and waistline, he commented that "from here on down she is going to be no different than the man" and he proceeded to give her what he identified as slacks.

The female figure is made larger, has a proportionately larger head than the male, is given a larger area of hair, and firm, aquiline features (*more authority, social domi-*

*nance, virility, and self assurance are ascribed to the female
—commonly seen in drawings of infantile male adults).*
The figure is more centrally placed and she is not in need
of the ground support given the male (*more aggressive
and secure*). The mouth is given some emphasis in both
figures (*oral concentration of subject*). Although he first
intended to draw the figure in profile, his need to exhibit
the breasts made a consistent profile of the figure untenable
(*fantasy undoubtedly fixed basically on the breasts with
avoidance of sexuality on a mature, genital level*).

With such problems as immaturity, virtual paralysis of
enterprise, and increasing withdrawal into body sensitivity,
the question as to the normality of this subject could be
raised. The problems presented by him are in the nature
of chronic personality deviations that are not uncommon
in our competitive society. No pathological withdrawal
is indicated. There is no evidence that the inner aggression will get out of control in a normal environment.
Logical thought is sustained, though productivity is hampered by indecision and obsessive traits. Though no overt
anxiety is evident, tension and superficial insight are felt.
Prognosis for a satisfactory sexual and marital adjustment
depends upon the type of mate selected. The subject shows
no overweaning ambition, self-esteem, or narcissism that
might clash with his actual lack of achievement to produce
a serious crisis. Also, the facilitation of the environment,
and the pressures that will be exerted upon him must be
considered in evaluating future adjustment.

BIBLIOGRAPHY

1. Anastasi, A. and Foley, J. P., Jr.: A survey of the literature on artistic behavior in the abnormal: III. Spontaneous productions. *Psychol. Monogr.*, *52:* 71, 1940.

2. Anastasi, A. and Foley, J. P., Jr.: A survey of the literature on artistic behavior in the abnormal: II. Approaches and interrelationships. *Ann. N.Y. Acad. Sci.*, *42:* 166, 1941.

3. Anastasi, A. and Foley, J. P., Jr.: A survey of the literature on artistic behavior in the abnormal: I. Historical and theoretical background. *J. Gen. Psychol.*, *25:* 111-132, 1941.

4. Anastasi, A. and Foley, J. P., Jr.: A survey of the literature on artistic behavior in the abnormal: IV. *Experimental Investigations. J. Gen. Psychol.*, *25:* 187-237, 1941.

5. Bender, Lauretta: Art and therapy in mental disturbances of children. *J. Nerv. & Ment. Dis.*, *86:* 249-263, 1937.

6. Bender, Lauretta: The Goodenough test in chronic encephalitis in children. *J. Nerv. & Ment. Dis.*, *91:* 277-286, 1940.

7. Brown and Goetein. Significance of body image for personality. *J. Nerv. & Ment. Dis.*, *97:* 401-408, 1943.

8. Cameron, N.: Individual and social factors in development of graphic ability. *J. Psychol.*, *5:* 165-184, 1938.

9. Despert, J. Louise: Emotional Problems in Children. Utica, State Hospitals Press, 1938.

10. Despert, J. Louise: Technical problems in the study of emotional problems in children. *Psychiat. Quart.*, 10, 1936.

11. Dunlap, Knight: The development and function of clothing. *J. Gen. Psych.*, *1:* 64, 1928.

12. Federn, P.: Narcissism in the structure of the ego. *Internat. J. Psycho-Analysis, 9:* 401, 1928.

13. Freud, S.: *New Introductory Lectures in Psychoanalysis.* New York, Norton, 1938.
14. Flugel, J. C.: Clothes symbolism and clothes ambivalence. *Internat. J. Psycho-Analysis, 10:* 205, 1929.
15. Flugel, J. C.: *Psychology of Clothing.* London, 1930.
16. Goodenough, F. L.: *Measurement of Intelligence by Drawings.* Yonkers, World Book Co., 1926.
17. Goodenough, F. L.: Studies in the psychology of children's drawings. *Psych. Bull., 25:* 272-283, 1928.
18. Guttman, E.: Clinical observations on schizophrenic drawings. *Brit. J. M. Psych., 16:* 1937.
19. Jones, E.: *Papers on Psychoanalysis.* London, 1918.
20. Levy, D.: Body interest in children. *Am. J. Psychiat., 12:* 295, 1932.
21. Lewis, N.: Graphic art productions in schizophrenia. *Research Nerv. & Ment. Dis., 5:* 344-368, 1928.
22. Machover, S.: *Cultural and Racial Variations in Patterns of Intellect.* New York, T. C. Contributions to Education. No. 875. 1943.
23. Orenstein and Schilder: Psychological considerations of insulin treatment. *J. Nerv. Ment. Dis., 88:* 397-413, 644-660, 1938.
24. Ross, N.: The postural model of the head and the face. *J. Gen. Psychol., 7:* 144, 1932.
25. Sanborn, H. C.: The function of clothing and adornment. *Am. J. Psychiat., 38:* 1, 1927.
26. Schilder, P.: Organic problems in child guidance. *Ment. Hyg., 15:* 480, 1931.
27. Schilder, P.: *The Image and Appearance of the Human Body.* London, 1935.
28. Schilder and Levine: Abstract art as an expression of human problems. *J. Nerv. & Ment. Dis., 96:* 1, 1942.
29. Schmidl, W. T.: Formal criteria for the analysis of childrens' drawings. *Am. J. Ortho. Psychiat., 12:* 95-104, 1942.
30. Wolff, W.: *The Expression of Personality.* New York, Harper, 1943.

INDEX

A

D

Deaf people, 26, 47
Dependence
  breast emphasis, 14, 99, 112, 156
  buckle in, 89, 114, 139, 146
  buttons in, 44, 78, 89, 126, 139, 155
  symbol of, 120
  head as organ of, 38
  midline emphasis and, 78, 89, 121, 126
  mother, 124, 126, 132, 135, 139, 141, 151, 155
  mouth, concave and receptive type, 44, 129
  pockets in, 79, 80, 126
Depersonalization fears, thick, heavy lines, 95
Depressed
  arms may be omitted, 62
  detailing may be abundant, 91
  erasures infrequent in retarded types, 98
  head emphasis in, 36
  mouth emphasis or omission of, 43
  placement, low on page, 89
  seated figure may be drawn, 65
  size of figure may be small, 91
Deprivation
  material, pocket emphasis, 70, 126
  oral, breast emphasis, 14, 70, 99, 112, 156, 157
Detailing
  empty, 91, 118
  female more, 132
  inessentials stressed, 65, 118, 121, 124
  meagre, 129, 145
  obsessive, 81, 119, 121, 130, 150, 154
  overdetailing, 12, 14, 37, 113, 119, 124, 130
Developmental considerations, 102-103
  head and legs "person," 39, 68, 102, 103
  mouth, concave, 8, 44, 129
  perspective, poor, 103

shading, 103
transparencies, 103
Diagrammatic quality, 87, 119
Differential between male and female, 100-102
  arms longer in female, 150
    omitted only in mother-figure, 62, 121
  attitudes toward sexes basic in, 102
  confusion of sexual characteristics, 48, 58, 67, 71, 101, 111, 114, 120
  defect, projection of on opposite sex, 55, 100
  erasures at same point, 111
  female more extraverted, 140
  hair on female, hat on male, 53, 82
  neat and messy, 53, 127
  head, large in, 38, 121, 132
  inconsistent with associations, 118, 127, 130, 149
  male in profile, female in front view, 94, 100, 129
  masculine drive in female, weaker male, 100, 145
  mother-son relationship, 138
  neck longer in female, 132
  treatment differential, 58, 132, 140
  overdressing and underdressing in one set, 77
  projection of traits on which figure?, 101
  trunk omitted in same sex and given to opposite, 68
  weak male, strong female, 12, 17, 53, 89, 113, 120, 132, 137, 156, 157
Differential diagnosis
  check list of traits, none, stress on patterns, 21, 104
  defective or organic vs. hysterical psychopath, 92
  established by drawings, 118, 132
  previous efforts, 19
Directions for drawing, 28-29
  associations for, 29

G

H

I

O

P

trousers on legs, 13, 74
Trunk, 68-69
    different shape for male and fe-
        male of a set, 68
    incomplete contour, 69
    oblong, square, or circle, 68
    omitted seldom in adults, 68
    offered as person, never, 39
    positional location on leg lines,
        68

U

Unconscious, 9, 10, 12, 89

V

Validation
    blind analysis, 25, 51, 104
    checks with competent opinion,
        24
    constant progress, in, 21, 83, 105
    matched sets of drawings with
        case histories, 26
    principles repeatedly verified in

clinical usage, 25, 103
Voyeurism
    case, 109-116
    eye, small, 49, 153
    transparency of female, 17, 157
    V neckline, 18

W

Waistline, 72-74
    belt, elaborate, 73
    clothing, as only index of, 72
    delay or impatience in handling,
        73
    disturbed or reinforced line, 18,
        66, 73, 120, 139
    tightened, 73
Withdrawal (see Schizoid), 42,
        112, 140, 147
Writing, spontaneous, 141
    titling, 15

Z

"Zoning" of body, 72-73